Mary I: Queen of England

A Tudor Times Insight

By Tudor Times

Published by Tudor Times Ltd

Tudor Times Insights

Tudor Times Insights are books collating articles from our website www.tudortimes.co.uk which is a repository for a wide variety of information about the Tudor and Stewart period 1485 – 1625. There you can find material on People, Places, Daily Life, Military & Warfare, Politics & Economics and Religion. The site has a Book Review section, with author interviews and a book club. It also features comprehensive family trees, and a 'What's On' event list with information about forthcoming activities relevant to the Tudors and Stewarts.

Titles in the Series

Profiles

People

Politics & Economy

Contents

Preface

Mary I was the first woman to rule England in her own right, with all the power and majesty of any previous King. The only surviving child of Henry VIII and Katharine of Aragon, Mary had a happy and privileged childhood, before she was thrust aside by the marriage of Henry to Anne Boleyn and forced to agree she was illegitimate. Returned to the succession by Parliamentary Act in 1544, there was an attempt to block her accession that she resisted with spirit and determination. Unfortunately, memories of the more successful aspects of her reign are overshadowed by the remembrance of religious persecution.

This book contains Mary I's Life Story and additional articles about her, looking at different aspects of her life. Mary owned one of the most celebrated natural pearls ever found, a gift related to the marriage that, in retrospect, has been seen as a disaster.

The material was first published on www.tudortimes.co.uk

Family Tree

Mary I
Queen of England

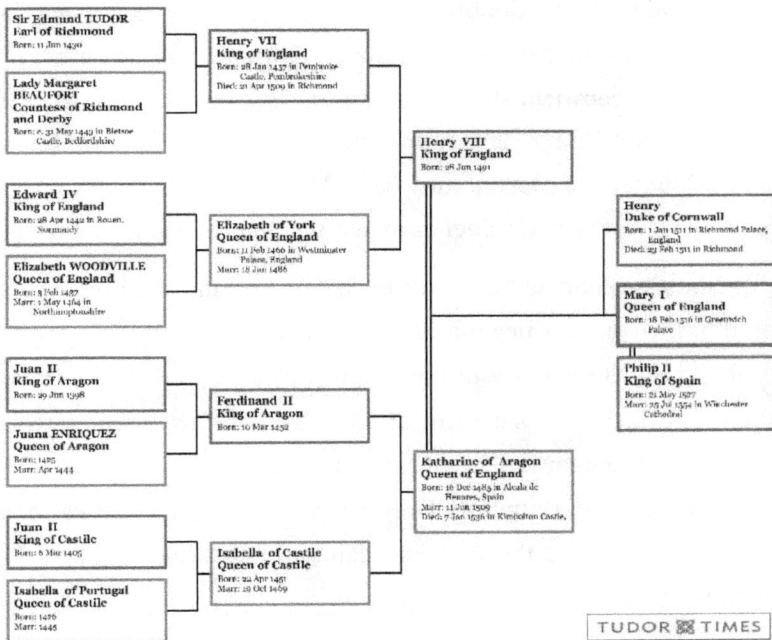

Sir Edmund TUDOR **Earl of Richmond** Born: 11 Jun 1430			
	Henry VII **King of England** Born: 28 Jan 1457 in Pembroke Castle, Pembrokeshire Died: 21 Apr 1509 in Richmond		
Lady Margaret **BEAUFORT** **Countess of Richmond** **and Derby** Born: c. 31 May 1443 in Bletsoe Castle, Bedfordshire			

Henry VIII
King of England
Born: 28 Jun 1491

Edward IV **King of England** Born: 28 Apr 1442 in Rouen, Normandy		**Henry** **Duke of Cornwall** Born: 1 Jan 1511 in Richmond Palace, England Died: 23 Feb 1511 in Richmond
	Elizabeth of York **Queen of England** Born: 11 Feb 1466 in Westminster Palace, England Marr: 18 Jan 1486	
Elizabeth WOODVILLE **Queen of England** Born: 3 Feb 1437 Marr: 1 May 1464 in Northamptonshire		**Mary I** **Queen of England** Born: 18 Feb 1516 in Greenwich Palace

Philip II
King of Spain
Born: 21 May 1527
Marr: 25 Jul 1554 in Winchester Cathedral

Juan II **King of Aragon** Born: 29 Jun 1398		
	Ferdinand II **King of Aragon** Born: 10 Mar 1452	
Juana ENRIQUEZ **Queen of Aragon** Born: 1425 Marr: Apr 1444		

Katharine of Aragon
Queen of England
Born: 16 Dec 1485 in Alcalá de Henares, Spain
Marr: 11 Jun 1509
Died: 7 Jan 1536 in Kimbolton Castle,

Juan II **King of Castile** Born: 6 Mar 1405		
	Isabella of Castile **Queen of Castile** Born: 22 Apr 1451 Marr: 18 Oct 1469	
Isabella of Portugal **Queen of Castile** Born: 1428 Marr: 1445		

Part 1: Mary I's Life Story

Chapter 1: Childhood (1516 – 1525)

Mary was the first of her parents' children to survive more than a few weeks, and was thus doubly precious to them, both as a living daughter, and as a sign of brothers to come. Born at the favoured palace of Placentia, Greenwich, she was baptised a few days later at the Church of the Observant Friars. Her godmothers were her great-aunt, Katherine of York, Countess of Devon, and Lady Margaret Plantagenet, Countess of Salisbury. Her father's chief minister, Cardinal Wolsey, was godfather.

Almost as soon as Mary was born, she became a valuable pawn to be used in the complex negotiations that Henry VIII and Wolsey carried out to maintain the balance of power in Europe – playing off François I of France against Mary's cousin, Charles, King of Spain. Aged two, Mary's first appearance on the European stage was at her betrothal to François I's oldest son, the Dauphin. Dressed in cloth of gold, she was held up by Cardinal Wolsey as the massive diamond betrothal ring was placed on her baby finger.

At the time, Mary's mother, Katharine of Aragon, was pregnant, and, optimistic that the coming child would be a boy, Henry had agreed with the French that, should Mary be his only child, she would inherit the throne. Unfortunately for both Henry and Katharine, the Queen's last pregnancy ended in another loss. The Venetian ambassador believed that, had Henry thought there was a real prospect of Mary inheriting, he would not have gone ahead with the betrothal.

Nevertheless, the agreement continued, and two years later, still promised to the Dauphin, Mary was left in nominal charge of the kingdom as her parents travelled to France to the Field of Cloth of Gold. In their absence, the French sent ambassadors to see her – presumably to check on her health and appearance. Apparently, Mary spoke up prettily and asked for strawberries to be served to the visitors. Her prospective mother-in-law, Queen Claude, also sent personal messengers to enquire after her.

Mary's education was the best available in the early 1520s to enlightened parents who were both well-educated themselves and patrons of the expanding Humanist ideal. Mary was taught Latin, French, history, philosophy, and mathematics as well as all the usual courtly accomplishments of music, needlework, dancing and outdoor pursuits including hunting, falconry and archery. At a later date she is noted as having some knowledge of Italian and Spanish, but it is unclear whether she studied them formally in childhood.

The Spanish humanist Juan-Luis Vives, although he was not her actual tutor, drew up a programme of education that was intended to turn her into a model of feminine virtue. It was, of course, still envisaged that Mary would be the wife of a King, rather than a Queen-Regnant herself.

In 1522, Henry's plans for Mary became even grander than a future as Queen of France. Her cousin, Charles of Spain, had been elected as Holy Roman Emperor. Keen to have English support in the interminable struggle between the Hapsburgs and the Valois Kings of France, Charles visited England twice, and it was agreed that he would marry Mary. She would be sent to Spain when she was twelve, and Henry, although unhappy that he had no son, could at least contemplate the thought that his grandson might become Emperor.

Chapter 2: Princess of Wales (1525 – 1531)

As the years passed and no more living children were born to Henry and Katharine, Mary's importance as a possible inheritor of the Crown of England increased. By 1525, with no legitimate male heir, Henry was torn between naming Mary, or her illegitimate half-brother, Henry FitzRoy, as his successor. Mary was sent to Ludlow, to preside over the Prince's Council in Wales as previous Princes of Wales had done. Although Mary never received the title formally, she was frequently referred to as Princess of Wales, whilst FitzRoy received the semi-regal titles of Duke of Richmond and Somerset, and President of the Council of the North.

During Mary's period in Ludlow, her household was presided over by her Lady Governess, the Countess of Salisbury, with John Dudley, later Duke of Northumberland, as Chamberlain. Her education continued, now with a wider curriculum that included more history and other topics considered important for rulers. The rules for her household were carefully laid down – she was to eat only good food, be surrounded by courteous and well-trained servants, to exercise regularly and not to study or practice her music to a point of fatigue.

During this period, she divided her time between the great castle of Ludlow, the manor of Bewdley (sometimes also called Beaulieu or Tickenhill), and the enormous Thornbury Castle, which had been confiscated from its previous owner, the Duke of Buckingham, following his execution in 1521. She also returned to London to see her parents at least once. During this period, Mary's chief Latin tutor was Dr

Fetherstone. Her mother wrote to Mary, saying that she would still like to receive copies of Mary's Latin exercises to monitor her progress.

On 24th February 1525, the Imperial victory over France at the Battle of Pavia transformed Mary's life, although she would not have known it at the time and might never have associated the defeat of France, something in which the English rejoiced, with the disasters which followed. Charles V, Mary's betrothed, having won a resounding victory over François I, no longer needed an English alliance, and in 1526, he broke off his betrothal to Mary to marry their mutual cousin, the fabulously wealthy Isabella of Portugal. Henry VIII was furious – betrayed by a man he had treated as his nephew, his daughter humiliated, and England revealed as no more than a bit-player in European politics.

The Spanish alliance, which had seemed to promise so much in 1489 when it had been forged by Henry's father and Katharine's parents, was now revealed as worthless. Katharine had not given him a son (in Tudor minds, fertility and obstetric issues were largely a woman's fault) and now her nephew had double crossed him – much as her father had done twice before. It was time to rethink English policy.

The Empire was riding too high and so alliance with France must be considered. Mary's betrothal to the Dauphin was not revived, instead, she was promised to François' second son, Henri, Duke of Orleans, who, as he was only eight, could not be expected to marry for six years. Then in an extraordinary twist of diplomacy, to François himself. Whilst the latter idea might sound repugnant, as François was 32 to Mary's eleven and a notorious lecher, it had the merit that any child Mary had by him would be monarch only of England, as François' heirs were his sons by Queen Claude. This would minimise the period of subjection to France that would inevitably follow the marriage, if Mary became Queen of England.

The treaty was agreed in 1527, and Mary was brought to London to take part in the accompanying celebrations. Her father, proud of her, pulled off the cap hiding her hair, to show a *'profusion of silver tresses'*. Nevertheless, the French ambassadors reported home that Mary was so slight in build that she could not possibly be married for at least three years.

Shortly after this betrothal, Henry VIII came up with a much better solution – in his own mind at least – to the problem of an heir. He sought an annulment of his marriage to Katharine of Aragon, who was now useless, both politically and personally, in Henry's eyes, in order to marry a young woman of the court, Anne Boleyn, with whom he had fallen violently in love, certain she would provide a male heir.

Katharine resisted the annulment with every fibre of her being – part of her reason was, presumably, her desire to protect Mary's inheritance. Although children of parents whose marriages were subsequently annulled were usually treated as legitimate if the parents had married in good faith, Katharine was well aware that any children of a second wife would be placed above Mary in the succession. For her to accept the annulment would not only deprive her daughter of her inheritance, but might also make her unmarriageable to a King.

Over the following years, as the annulment suit dragged on interminably, Mary's day to day life continued much as before, although in and around the court in London, rather than in Wales, and in May 1528 she spent a month with both parents at the palace of Tittenhanger, where Henry had retired to avoid the plague stalking the capital. Although her household was slightly reduced, Lady Salisbury remained in charge of it, and her lessons and recreations carried on smoothly.

Henry remained attached to his daughter, and perhaps hoped that, if the annulment were granted, she would accept the situation and take her place as an illegitimate, but loved child, much as the Duke of Richmond did. Mary pleaded to see more of the King, and spent a whole day with her father in July 1530, at Richmond, but, as time passed, Anne became nervous that Henry's affection for his daughter would make him less eager to pursue the annulment and discouraged such visits.

She need not have feared – Henry was bent on marrying her, and Mary's blatant disobedience was beginning to irk him. Although only in her teens, Mary made her support of her mother quite clear. She was an intelligent and educated girl, and would have been well aware of the threat to her own position, but we cannot doubt that her support for her mother was a product of sincere love. Nevertheless, for a girl to disobey not just her father but her king, was an almost unimaginable act in an era when obedience to fathers was considered the pre-eminent duty, even of grown men. Failure to make his adolescent daughter conform reflected badly on Henry's prestige.

Henry, not surprisingly, although mistakenly, concluded that once separated from her mother, Mary would accept his decision that her parents' marriage was invalid, so in the summer of 1531, the two were parted, never to meet again. Shortly after, aged fifteen, Mary fell ill, with sickness and stomach problems. Although she wrote to her father that seeing her mother would be her best cure, this was not permitted. Her public status, however, remained the same, and she granted an audience to the Venetian Ambassador who described her as small, but pretty and with a lovely complexion. He also praised her linguistic and musical skills.

Two years later, on the birth of Anne's daughter, Elizabeth, Mary's status was radically altered. Her rank was degraded from Princess to merely *'the Lady Mary, the King's daughter'*, and her household was disbanded. Lady Salisbury offered to remain and maintain the Princess' household at her own expense, but this offer was rejected – Henry believing that Lady Salisbury was stiffening his daughter's disobedience. Mary was to join the new baby at Hatfield, as her attendant. Mary had no choice but to go, protesting bitterly that she was still her father's only legitimate child and heir, although, she added (whether sarcastically or in a misguided effort to seem accommodating) that, since Henry acknowledged Elizabeth as his, she would call her *'sister'* as she called Richmond *'brother'*.

Her sojourn at Hatfield was deeply humiliating for Mary as she was subject to petty restrictions and bullying. She was not permitted to walk in the gardens, or to attend the parish church, or even the public gallery of the house, lest she attract public support. Her jewels were confiscated and her clothes were not replaced. Her mother had a letter smuggled to her, in which she warned Mary not to disobey her father, other than in matters which might imperil her soul, but not to enter into disputes or arguments. She was to keep herself chaste and, in a word of practical warning, keep her keys personally – presumably to prevent anyone slipping treasonable papers into her desk.

This oppressive treatment for a girl used to nothing but love and respect told severely on Mary's health, and she remained of a delicate constitution, prone to what were probably stress-related illnesses, for the rest of her life. She suffered migraines, stomach problems, and what sounds to modern ears like allergic reactions – perhaps hay-fever. Nevertheless, she refused to give in and would not, by any word or action, accept the downgrading in her status or her mother's marriage. During this period, she did not see her father face-to-face as, on his visits to Hatfield, she was confined to her room. On one occasion, as the King and his entourage was about to depart, she ran up onto the roof, and, his attention drawn to her by one of his courtiers, Henry, looking up and doffed his cap to her, with all of his train following suit. Later, although he defended his refusal to see his daughter, on account of her obstinacy, there were tears in his eyes.

In 1534, the Pope finally pronounced on the annulment case – his judgement was too little, too late. His confirmation of the validity of Henry and Katharine's marriage, and his injunction to Henry to banish Anne, and return to Katharine, fell on deaf ears. The English Parliament confirmed that Henry and Anne's marriage was legal, and that Elizabeth was heir to the throne. Refusal to sign the Oath of Succession and the later Oath of Supremacy (which made Henry Head of the Church in England) was considered treason, punishable by death.

Katharine refused the oaths, and in January 1535, Mary was informed that she too would be served with them. Perhaps the stress this threat occasioned was the trigger, as a couple of weeks later, Mary fell seriously ill. Despite a series of pleading letters from Katharine, she was not permitted to be nursed by her mother, although Henry sent his own doctors and allowed Katharine's doctor to attend her as well – perhaps to quash rumours of poisoning.

Somewhat recovered, towards the end of the year, Mary sent secret messages to the Imperial Ambassador, Eustache Chapuys, asking him to help her escape an intolerable situation, as the likelihood of being asked to swear the oaths loomed closer. Catching wind of the plan, the Government ensured that security was increased at Hatfield and the ports were watched.

In January 1536, Mary's mother died. She was not permitted to attend the funeral, nor did she receive the bequests of furs that Katharine made in her will. Mary's importance was less, in the eyes of the Emperor, than Katharine's had been, and, as François was by now resurgent in Europe, Charles was soon making appeasing noises to Henry.

Anne, having initially rejoiced in Katharine's death, began to feel the cold winds of the loss of Henry's favour. She made conciliatory gestures towards Mary, saying that, if her step-daughter would only submit and recognise Anne's and Elizabeth's positions, Anne would be like another mother to her, Mary could come to court, and would not even be obliged to carry Anne's train. Mary rejected the offer with disdain, and, pregnant again, Anne sent a message washing her hands of Mary – adding that, once her son was born,

'I (Anne) know what will happen to her (Mary)', which many interpreted as a threat.

In February, Henry appeared to be relenting in his treatment of his daughter. He had fallen in love with Jane Seymour, one of Anne Boleyn's ladies-in-waiting, and formerly a member of Katharine's household. Jane was sympathetic to Mary, and perhaps it was her influence that encouraged Henry to give Mary a large sum of money to distribute in alms as she and Elizabeth travelled between palaces.

By May, Anne Boleyn had been executed, and Jane was Queen in her place. Mary, who, as was natural, had blamed Anne entirely for her treatment, rather than her father, obviously hoped to be reconciled with Henry, writing a series of desperately supplicatory letters, first to Thomas Cromwell, Henry's chief minister, then to the King himself. She promised she would be as obedient as could be *'reasonably required'*, but there was no let-up in the pressure placed on her to accept both the Royal Supremacy over the Church and that her parents' marriage had been invalid. A delegation, headed by the Duke of Norfolk came to Hunsdon with orders to make sure she submitted. She still refused. The delegation, leaving orders for her to be locked in her room, departed.

Next, those courtiers who were known to be sympathetic towards her were arrested and questioned about their support for the Princess. Several were cast into the Tower of London, and it seemed only a matter of time before Mary joined them.

She had received a secret reassurance that the Pope would grant absolution from her oath if she signed under duress, so in June 1522, aged twenty, browbeaten, terrified and perhaps feeling guilty over the suffering that support of her was causing others, Mary gave in, and accepted both that her parents' marriage was invalid and that Henry was the Supreme Head of the Church.

Chapter 3: Back in Favour (1536 – 1547)

Henry was overjoyed at Mary's capitulation, both as confirming his royal authority that had been undermined by her disobedience, and also as a father, fond of his little girl, and hurt by her refusal to accept his will. Mary was given clothes, jewels and money, offered her choice of servants (with the exception of Lady Salisbury) and brought within weeks to Hackney to be reconciled with Henry, whom she hadn't seen for five long years.

Mary re-joined the court, taking precedence over everyone except the new Queen Jane Seymour, with whom she soon formed a warm relationship. There was one more thing for her to do to prove her submission – she must write to her cousin, Mary of Hungary, the Regent of the Netherlands (sister of Emperor Charles), confirming her acceptance of her illegitimate status and Henry's ecclesiastical supremacy. She did as required, but secretly requested absolution from the Pope. Mary was playing a dangerous game – had Henry discovered her duplicity, she might well have ended up in the Tower, or perhaps even on the scaffold.

Fortunately, Henry was satisfied and Mary was treated with affection and honour, although she was not restored to the succession in the act of 1536 which also barred Elizabeth from inheritance. The rebellion known as the Pilgrimage of Grace, which began in October of 1536, had, as one of its stated aims, the restoration of Mary to the succession, but despite the participation and execution of Sir John Hussey, who had once been her Lord Steward, Mary was not suspected of any involvement. She spent the Christmas of 1536 at court, and must have witnessed Henry's treatment of the rebel leader, Robert Aske, as practically a long-lost brother, whilst he awaited the opportunity to destroy him.

In the following spring, it was suggested to Henry that Mary might be declared legitimate so that she could make a marriage of alliance, but, with a pregnant Queen, Henry refused. Mary returned to Hampton Court in the summer of that year to witness the birth of Jane's son, Edward. On 15th October she stood as god-mother to her half-brother, giving him a golden cup, which he presumably valued once he was older, and the munificent sum of £30 to be shared by his nurse and other attendants.

The rejoicing in Edward's birth was soon overtaken by sorrow for the death of Queen Jane. Mary was so overcome with grief for her kind step-mother that she was unable to take part in the initial mourning duties, but was sufficiently recovered to act as Chief Mourner, following the Queen's hearse to Windsor, on a horse draped in black.

Mary was more than twenty years older than the baby, and for the first years of his life was the nearest he had to a mother, visiting him regularly in the nursery palace at Richmond, and making him frequent presents. Despite her earlier rejection of Elizabeth's legitimacy, she was also kind-hearted enough to plead for the little girl, who was now sadly neglected.

With Henry widowed, and Mary marriageable, the late 1530s were a period of negotiation for marital alliances – she was postulated again as a bride for Henri of Orleans, and also for Dom Luis of Portugal. Unfortunately, neither gentleman was willing to take a bride who was not legitimate and Henry was adamant that she was only his 'natural' daughter.

1538 was a difficult year – the ramifications of the Exeter Conspiracy resulted in the deaths of Henry Pole, Lord Montague, who was the son of Mary's former Governess, Lady Salisbury, as well as her cousin, the Marquess of Exeter, whose wife, Gertrude was a close friend of Mary's. Sir Nicholas Carew, too, once a friend of Queen Jane, was executed. They had all been supporters of Mary and her mother.

By 1539, Henry was looking for an alliance with which he could counter the unusual and unwelcome rapprochement between François and the Emperor Charles. Encouraged by Cromwell, who had Lutheran leanings, Henry sought an alliance with the Schmalkaldic League, led by the Lutheran Elector of Saxony. The plan was for Henry to marry the Elector's sister-in-law, Anne of Cleves, and for Mary to marry Anne's brother, Duke Wilhelm of Cleves. Mary was described as full of beauty, learning and virtue, even though she was only Henry's illegitimate daughter.

No match with Duke Wilhelm was agreed, but a second suitor actually visited in person – Duke Philip of Bavaria. Mary met him in person, and he seemed eager to marry her – even taking the liberty of kissing her, which gave rise to rumours that a wedding would swiftly follow. Whether

Mary could have been persuaded to marry a man who was openly Lutheran is debatable, but, in any event, Henry had no intention of letting any match take place.

Meanwhile, the King himself married Anne of Cleves. Mary was the foremost of the court ladies in all of the celebrations arranged to welcome the new Queen. She maintained a good relationship with her, even after Henry, completely unable to stomach marital life with Anne, whom he found physically unattractive, had the marriage annulled. Fortunately for him, the alliance between France and the Empire soon collapsed, and the need for an alliance with the Lutheran princes had diminished. It was less fortunate for Cromwell, who was executed.

No doubt Henry's infatuation with one of Anne's maids-of-honour, Katheryn Howard, also influenced his decision to have the marriage annulled. He and Katheryn were married in July 1540. This was difficult for Mary. Katheryn was at least five years her junior, and was also first cousin to Anne Boleyn. The new Queen felt that her step-daughter was not showing her the respect that was her due. Mary quickly mended her ways, and with the easy generosity that seems to have been a hallmark of Katheryn's character, her step-daughter was invited to reside permanently at court.

Despite the seemingly happy family atmosphere, Mary had to accept the death of Lady Salisbury in May 1541. The sixty-nine year old countess, niece of Edward IV and Richard III, had been held in the Tower since 1539, and was now executed without trial. Her last words were prayers for Henry, Katheryn, Edward and Mary.

By October of that year, Queen Katheryn was being investigated by Archbishop Cranmer and the Council when it emerged that, prior to her marriage, she had had sexual relationships with both her music master, and a distant relative, Francis Dereham. The investigations revealed that the young Queen had also been indulging in a relationship with a gentleman of Henry's Privy Chamber, Thomas Culpeper. It was debatable whether Katheryn had actually committed adultery, but if the act had not been committed by the time of her arrest, it was certainly the most likely eventual outcome of her secret meetings with the young man.

Katheryn was executed, and Henry, with no new queen in sight, turned to his elder daughter for a female figurehead for the court. He gave her expensive gifts of jewellery, and had apartments fitted out for her at Hampton Court and Whitehall. Despite this favourable treatment, Mary suffered from intermittent ill-health – stomach problems, palpitations of the heart and fevers being amongst the symptoms.

By 1543, recovered from whatever had ailed her, Mary was again presiding over the court, and, in her train was Katherine Parr, the widowed Lady Latimer. In July of that year, Lady Latimer became Mary's fourth and final step-mother in a ceremony that Mary attended, together with her half-sister, Elizabeth, and her cousin and friend, Lady Margaret Douglas.

Throughout her period as Queen, Katherine Parr treated Mary honourably and with true friendship. They had many intellectual tastes in common, as well as a shared love of music and fine clothes.

Katherine was of a literary, as well as of an evangelical turn of mind, and patronised the translation into English of Erasmus' Paraphrases on the Gospels. She persuaded Mary, an accomplished Latinist, to translate the Paraphrase of the Gospel of St John. Ill again, during the autumn of 1544, Mary was unable to complete the work, but it was under her name that it was published with the other translations.

Mary's warm relationship with her half-brother also thrived. He wrote to Katherine, exhorting her to protect Mary from the wiles of the devil, manifested in the princess' enjoyment of *foreign dances and*

merriments which do not become a most Christian princess.' He also
wrote to Mary herself, gravely informing her that although he did not
write to her often, he loved her most, just as he loved his best clothes
most, although he did not wear them all the time. Mary's relationship
with Elizabeth was never so close, although she continued to give the
younger girl expensive gifts.

In the Parliamentary session of 1543-44, a new Succession Act was
passed, in which Mary was named as successor to Edward, should he
have no children, to be followed by Elizabeth, should she herself have no
heirs. In an unprecedented step, Parliament also gave Henry the right to
appoint any successor to follow his three children.

On 28th January 1547, Henry died. It is unlikely that Mary saw him in
his last weeks. She and Queen Katherine had spent Christmas together,
at Greenwich, but Henry had remained at Whitehall.

Mary was well provided for by the terms of her father's will. It
confirmed her place in the succession, although on the proviso that she
could not marry without the consent of a majority of the members of the
Council he had instituted to govern during the minority of Edward. In
addition, she received an income of £3,000 and a dowry of £10,000 (not
so generous as the £50,000 her grandfather had left for his daughter's
marriage), as well as household plate and goods.

In Europe, there was some question as to whether Edward was the
legitimate King. Since he had been born after England's breach with
Rome, there were many Catholics who considered Mary, rather than
Edward, as Henry's legitimate heir. Mary made no challenge to her
brother, immediately accepting him as King. Perhaps in recognition of
this, when the new Privy Councillors interpreted Henry's will in a way
that resulted in huge land and money grants for themselves, Mary was
included in the bonanza, receiving a landed estate that made her one of

the richest magnates in England. Her estates were largely comprised of the Howard lands which had been confiscated from the Duke of Norfolk, now languishing in the Tower, and were concentrated in East Anglia.

Mary was, initially, at least, on good terms with the new Protector, Queen Jane's brother, Edward, quickly named as Duke of Somerset. She also seems to have been the only person in England to have a good word for his wife, Anne Stanhope, whom everyone else considered rude and overbearing.

Sadly, within weeks of Henry's death, a coolness sprang up between Mary and the Dowager Queen Katherine, when the latter secretly married Sir Thomas Seymour, another brother of Queen Jane. Mary was offended by this apparent disrespect towards her father, and retired to her new house at Kenninghall, in Norfolk. The two were reconciled at some point, although they did not meet again, and Mary sent Katherine encouraging letters during the Dowager Queen's pregnancy. The resulting baby, Mary Seymour, was named for Mary.

Chapter 4: Religious Differences (1547 – 1553)

Mary's willingness to be involved in the translation of Erasmus' Paraphrases in 1544 suggests that she was not so conservative in religion as to object to all reformation of the Church, a position borne out by the later concentration on a rejuvenated approach to Catholicism when she became Queen. Certainly, once she had accepted her father's Supremacy, she raised no objections to any of the religious modifications of his reign.

This acceptance, however, could not be maintained when the new Government, led by the Protestant Duke of Somerset, instituted sweeping changes. The Lutheran Book of Homilies and an English Bible were to be in every church, whilst the Lord's Prayer, Creed and the Ten Commandments were to be recited in English. One of the requirements was for the Paraphrases to be available in every parish church – we don't know whether Mary appreciated the irony of this. This was followed by the repeal of the traditionalist Act of Six Articles, permission for clergy to marry, and the injunction for communion to be received in both kinds (ie both bread and wine) by the lay congregation.

Mary wrote her objections to Somerset, contending, initially, that, as Edward was a minor (only nine on his father's death) he could not possibly opine maturely on religious doctrine, and that his role as Supreme Head of the Church could not be carried out by anyone else, not even Somerset. This was, of course, a legalistic objection, and Mary was careful not to say that she would reject any changes in religion that Edward might make when he was of age.

The Prayer Book of 1549, probably in the main the work of Thomas Cranmer, the Archbishop of Canterbury who had pronounced her parent's marriage as invalid, denied (by implication, although not in words) the doctrine of transubstantiation. This belief, that the bread and wine actually became the Body and Blood of Christ during the Mass, became the breaking point between Catholics and Protestants (although Luther had maintained the doctrine). This was a point beyond which no Catholic could go and when it became the only service that could be performed legally in an English church, Mary, and many other Catholics were horrified.

Mary requested the Emperor to intervene on her behalf, and he wrote to Somerset and the Council, assuring them that any attempt to prevent his cousin hearing the Mass would not be tolerated by him or any of her other relatives. Somerset, anxious to appease Charles, replied that, whilst Mary could not be exempted from the law of the land, and was subject to it, he would not make any close investigation into what might be happening behind closed doors in her own home. Rather than accepting this with good grace, Mary flagrantly abused what was intended as a personal privilege (she invited all and sundry to hear Mass in her Chapel).

Such open disobedience was unacceptable and the Council wrote to her insisting that she obey the law. She responded that the new law was not valid, as Edward was not of age, and Parliament had no authority in religious matters.

Mary was not the only one to object to the new service, and in 1549, the Prayer Book rebellion broke out in the South West as the men of Cornwall rejected the English service, which many of them could not understand. Simultaneously, although for economic rather than religious causes, there were uprisings in the east of England, led by Robert Kett. Mary was informed that some of her servants were involved in both uprisings, the implication being that she was complicit. This was a charge she hotly denied and no evidence was brought against her.

Protected by the Emperor, Mary became far more ostentatious in her religion than previously, hearing Mass more frequently and with more ceremony. Somerset, unsure what to do, and fearing foreign invasion, decided to ignore her, but Edward, who although barely entering his teens was becoming as hard-line a Protestant as Mary was Catholic, began to insist that Mary conform. Preachers and books were sent to her to show her the error of her ways, with complete lack of success.

Somerset was quite unable to manage the challenges of his office, and in September 1549 was overthrown by John Dudley, who had been

Mary's Lord Chamberlain in Ludlow nearly 25 years before. Now Earl of
Warwick, he became, not Protector, but the more-modest sounding
President of the Council.

Warwick had initially been supported by the more religiously
conservative Councillors, and the group had also requested support from
Mary, assuring the Imperial Ambassador that she would be permitted to
hear the Mass. Mary declined to involve herself in Council in-fighting.
She had no high opinion of Warwick, informing the Imperial
Ambassador that he was '*unstable*' of character, and motivated in his
coup by ambition and envy. Perhaps she did not trust the promises made
as to the freedom of worship she would be allowed and in that, she would
have been right. Warwick proved himself far more radically Protestant
than Somerset.

Invited to spend Christmas 1549 at court, with Edward and Elizabeth,
she declined the invitation, as she suspected it was made to prevent her
hearing Mass. She would visit after the religious season, staying at her
own house in London.

Pressure to conform increased, and Mary, despairing of her situation,
requested the Emperor's help to escape from a situation that was
increasingly intolerable. Eventually, in June 1550, the reluctant Charles
sent three ships for her, but, wracked with indecision, and discouraged
by her Comptroller, Richard Rochester, who exaggerated the risk of
capture, she changed her mind at the last minute, and stayed.

The Council now decided that the limits of tolerance for Mary's
flouting of the law had been reached. When her household heard Mass
without her being present, this was seized upon as a reason for
withdrawing any concessions made to her personally. Summoned to
court for Christmas 1550, she was taken to task by thirteen-year-old
Edward. She refused to accept that he was sufficiently mature to

pronounce on religious matters, whilst he insisted that she must obey his laws. They were both reduced to tears by their inability to find common ground.

In the following January, orders went out, absolutely forbidding her to hear Mass. Edward wrote to her personally, insisting that she must accept his laws, like any other subject, and in March 1551 she was again summoned to Court.

She arrived in London, making a demonstration, not just of her faith (her entire retinue was carrying the forbidden rosary) but also her power. Her train consisted of at least four hundred men and women, and was cheered as it processed from her house at Clerkenwell to Whitehall. Again she and Edward wrangled, to the distress of both.

Further intervention, and an outright threat of war from the Emperor, failed to persuade the Council to change course. A new alliance with France gave less weight to the Emperor's threats. Mary's chaplains were forbidden to say Mass, and security on the coast was stepped up to prevent her leaving the country. Mary could no longer hear Mass, and some of her household officers were sent to the Tower, but she refused to countenance the prescribed service in her house.

Later in 1551, with another outbreak of the Franco-Imperial war and fears that England might decide to support France, led Mary of Hungary, Regent of the Netherlands, to moot an invasion of England. This show of her cousin's power augured well for Mary, as, in an attempt to reduce the threat, she began to be treated with more respect. Her servants who had been arrested were released in March 1552, and that summer she was again invited to visit Edward at Greenwich.

The little brother she had doted on was now in less robust health that he had been, having suffered simultaneous bouts of measles and small pox. With the prospect that Mary might actually become Queen,

Edward's Councillors relaxed their attitude towards her, and again overlooked the saying of Mass for her, even whilst the 1552 Prayer Book, a far more radically Protestant service book than that of 1549, became the law of the land.

Chapter 5: Fighting for the Crown (1553)

In February 1553, Mary visited London. She again made a show of strength, and was met by Dudley, now Duke of Northumberland, and a phalanx of courtiers who accompanied her to Whitehall and treated her almost with the ceremony due to a monarch. Edward was too ill to see her for several days, but both Mary and Elizabeth were assured it was only a cold and that he would soon be better.

Over the next few months, a plot was hatched to deprive Mary of her inheritance. Whether the idea was genuinely Edward's or whether it had been suggested to him by Northumberland remains a moot point, but the upshot was that Edward drew up a 'device' for the succession, which would eliminate both Mary and Elizabeth, and replace them with their cousin, Lady Jane Grey, who, coincidentally or not, was married to Northumberland's son, Guilford.

The Council, with varying degrees of delight and reluctance, signed up to the Letters Patent through which Edward attempted to put his desire into law. The legality of the action was questionable – Edward was a minor, so could not make a will, and it had been long established that Letters Patent could not overturn a Parliamentary statute. Nevertheless, the plan went ahead, supported by promises of French military aid. For

Henri II (once Mary's betrothed) the prospect of an England ruled by the Emperor's cousin was to be avoided at all costs.

In early July 1553, Mary received word from London that Edward was ill and summoning her to attend him. Informed, though nobody knows by whom, of the plot against her, Mary left Hunsdon in the middle of the night, heading for her territories in East Anglia. En route, she stopped at Sawston Hall, owned by the Huddlestone family. After rising at dawn, hearing Mass and eating breakfast, she set off again, only hours before Northumberland's men arrived. The house was burnt to the ground by way of a warning to others not to support Mary.

Back in the capital, Jane had resisted pressure to accept the Crown initially, but was persuaded that it was her duty to accept it to protect the Protestant faith, although she was adamant that her husband would not be King.

On 7th July, Mary received reliable information that Edward was dead, and that Lady Jane had been proclaimed Queen. She raced on for the security of Kenninghall. From Kenninghall, Mary began the fight back. She wrote to the Council, demanding she be proclaimed Queen, and assuring them of forgiveness if they immediately behaved themselves. Instead of accepting her claims, the Council responded, offensively reminding Mary of her illegitimacy, and thus inability to inherit the Crown, but assuring her that, if she accepted Jane as Queen, they would be glad to be of service to her.

On 13th July, Northumberland marched out of London to capture Mary. No-one else had been willing to go, and Northumberland's parting words suggested that he had little trust in his fellow Councillors, but the defeatist Imperial Ambassador wrote gloomily to his master, that Mary was likely to be captured within days. The Emperor declined to send any practical assistance to her.

The day before Northumberland had left, to deafening silence from the London populace, Mary had transferred, with a growing multitude of supporters, to the great stronghold of Framlingham in Suffolk. She sent further letters to the Council and to the major cities, declaring her rights and demanding that she be proclaimed Queen immediately. Before long she had a sizeable army. A Lincolnshire man wrote to the Council:

'Her grace should have her right, or else there would be the bloodiest day...that ever was in England.'

Almost as soon as Northumberland had departed, the individual lords of the Council, having second thoughts, sent secret messages to Mary, assuring her of their support. At Framlingham, more men came in, together with the Earls of Bath and Surrey, the Lord Wentworth and many of the gentry of eastern England.

Mary prepared to fight, and on 20th July she spent three hours reviewing her troops. Soon news came that Northumberland had surrendered in Cambridge, perhaps, at the last, unwilling to return England to the civil wars of the previous century, or perhaps aware that he had no hope of vanquishing Mary's increasing army. News reached London that Mary had been proclaimed Queen throughout East Anglia. Heralds were immediately sent out by the members of the Council who had hurriedly remembered their loyalty, to St. Paul's, to proclaim her in the City. The bells were rung and bonfires lit in the streets.

Mary, flanked by her supporters, entered London in triumph, to a tumultuous public welcome. She was joined at Wanstead by her half-sister, Elizabeth, who had done nothing to aid either of the contending parties. Dressed in purple velvet and cloth of gold, and followed by a huge train of peers and their ladies, as well as by the Lord Mayor and a choir of children, Mary rode to the Tower of London. There, she was greeted by a couple of old adversaries from her father's reign, Thomas

Howard, 3rd Duke of Norfolk, and Stephen Gardiner, Bishop of Winchester, whom she named as Lord Chancellor.

Mary also found Edward Courtenay, who had been imprisoned since the Exeter Conspiracy of 1539. Aged 26, he had spent all of his youth incarcerated. His mother, Gertrude Blount, Marchioness of Exeter, had always been one of Mary's warmest supporters.

These prisoners were freed, but the Dukes and Duchesses of Suffolk and Northumberland, and the Lady Jane and Guilford Dudley, remained in the Tower, transferred from the royal apartments to respectable lodgings elsewhere, rather than dungeons.

In due course, the two Duchesses and Suffolk were pardoned, but Northumberland, despite a last minute reconversion to the Catholic faith, was executed, along with a couple of his lieutenants. Lady Jane and Guilford, having been found guilty of treason in a trial at the Guildhall, were detained in the Tower whilst Mary contemplated their fates.

The French were worried, and quickly denied having given any support to Northumberland and the Emperor hastily re-wrote history by telling his ambassador to inform Mary that he had been in the very midst of sending her aid when the good news of her bloodless succession had arrived.

On 1st October, Mary was crowned in Westminster Abbey, the first woman to be crowned as Queen Regnant in England (her young cousin, Mary, Queen of Scots had been crowned in Scotland some eleven years before.)

Chapter 6: Mary's Policy (1553 – 1554)

Mary, like any other monarch, needed a Privy Council. In a display of pragmatism, she took at face value the contrition of those who had begged forgiveness for any involvement in the attempted coup, and leavened their untrustworthiness by appointing some of the household officers who had served her since the 1530s.

She also, unwisely in hindsight, put far too much trust in Simon Renard, the Imperial Ambassador. Since, in Mary's mind, the Emperor had been her champion and protector for years, she believed that he continued to have her best interests at heart, but for Charles, his support of his cousin would always be subordinate to the best interests of his vast empire, and sometimes, what was good for the empire was not good for Mary. Nevertheless, she did not follow Renard's advice slavishly, an instance being her refusal to listen to his urgings to have Lady Jane and her husband executed.

The new Queen had two overwhelming ambitions – to restore the religious and social world to the lost Elysian Fields of her childhood, before her father had questioned his marriage to her mother, and to have an heir of her own. Both of these ambitions were within the realm of the possible as matters stood in 1553, but there were serious obstacles to their easy achievement.

To take the religious question first, the vast majority of the population, other than a small, but very vocal group in London and the south east, were still Catholic in their religious habits and inclinations. The situation as left at the death of Henry VIII was essentially one of Catholic practice, with some innovations around an English Bible, and, most radical of all, the removal of the Pope as the head of the Church.

Almost immediately, the banned altars and relics that had been hidden away reappeared, and a Latin Mass was sung in London.

This was not universally welcome in the capital, and a number of Protestant preachers began to incite rebellion. Mary was, of course, according to law, the Supreme Head of the Church. However, she did not use this power to immediately reintroduce Catholicism. Instead, she announced that, whilst she herself would not deny her own faith, there would be no compulsion in religious matters until Parliament had been called.

Mary did, however, immediately begin to put pressure on her half-sister to attend Mass and show herself a Catholic. Elizabeth, claiming that she had never been taught the old religion (which cannot be true, as she was thirteen at the time of her father's death, and both she and Edward had worshipped in conformity with the Act of Six Articles), asked for instruction. She soon aroused suspicions of her sincerity when she complained of stomach-aches during Mass or was prevented from attendance by minor illnesses.

The Parliament of late 1553 was happy to unravel the religious legislation of Edward's reign, reflecting the opinions of the majority of the population. This Parliament also repealed the Treason Acts which had been passed in Henry VIII's reign, returning the definition of treason to that of the Act of 1352 which required action against the monarch, rather than just verbal attacks.

The question of Papal Supremacy, however, was more difficult. To remember a time when the Pope was supreme, you had to be in your late thirties, in a time when a growing population meant that fifty per cent of the population was well under this age. There was plenty of enthusiasm for the return of the saints' days, the processions, the prayers for the dead and the ritual of the centuries, but there was little appetite for payment of taxes to a foreign power.

The other stumbling block, was the land distribution that had followed the dissolution of the monasteries. Even committed Catholics in religion had profited greatly from the land grab, and very few were willing to put their souls above their purses in this case.

For Mary, Papal Supremacy mattered, because, if the Pope had no spiritual power higher than that of other bishops, he could not have legitimately granted the dispensation for her parents' marriage. She would probably have been better advised to say nothing on the topic and just accept her position as Queen without concentrating on the whys and wherefores as Elizabeth was later to do. But Mary was not of a character to cope well with indecision, and, of course, she also genuinely believed in Papal Supremacy and the importance of a single, united Christendom under his leadership.

Some, such as her Lord Chancellor, Bishop Gardiner, who had been happy to deny Papal Supremacy in the 1530s, had come to the conclusion that only by having a central authority could fragmentation of religion be avoided, essential in an age that saw religious uniformity as absolutely necessary for the proper functioning of society.

Nevertheless, in this first Parliament, Papal Supremacy was not restored. Mary even took advantage of her position as Supreme Head (although she avoided use of the title) to lay down injunctions as to the conduct of services, and the deprivation of their sees from married priests who refused to abandon their wives.

The second item on the Queen's agenda, the getting of an heir, was just about practicable had she been in good health, but Mary had had menstrual difficulties all her adult life, was not particularly robust and was well over 37 when she became Queen. She needed to find a husband, get married and conceive in very short order to have any hope of an heir.

There was no shortage of candidates for her hand, and Mary's Councillors and subjects expected her to marry as soon as possible, not just because an heir was required, but because received wisdom was that women were not suited to being monarchs or in positions of power. This was not, of course, the day-to-day experience of most people, as, in all classes of life, women took an active part in managing businesses, arranging marriages, acting as their husband's partners and deputies and functioning independently when widowed. But although individual women were recognised as perfectly capable of managing affairs, the theory was rather different.

To clarify Mary's position as sovereign, it was enacted in her first Parliament that she had exactly the same authority as a male sovereign, and this was an understanding of her role from which Mary never deviated. But what would the position of her husband be? For other female heiresses, on marriage, the husband immediately owned all of her personal goods and possessions, and had a life interest in her lands. Similarly, it was thought that a Queen's husband would be King, for at least as long as she lived.

To marry one of her subjects would therefore cause enormous friction as one noble was elevated above the others. To marry a foreign prince risked Mary being taken abroad and England being devoured by his country. To remain unmarried, however, was not an option that anyone considered feasible, with the exception of Cardinal Reginald Pole. Pole, who had been exiled since the early 1530s, was the son of Mary's former Governess, Lady Salisbury, and had been named as Papal Legate to England by Pope Julius III, even before any decision had been made about returning to the Roman fold.

Mary had two marital options at home - the aforementioned Courtenay, who was the nearest male blood relative of the royal family of age to marry. But Courtenay had spent so much time in the Tower that he lacked the maturity and experience that Mary needed in a husband. The second home-grown candidate was Pole himself.

Despite being a Cardinal, Pole was not actually an ordained priest. He was in his early fifties and had been mentioned as an appropriate husband for Mary back in the 1530s, both by the rebels of the Pilgrimage of Grace, and the Exeter Conspiracy. However, Mary had a different role in mind for Pole. He was ordained priest and instituted as Archbishop of Canterbury, following the deprivation and death of Cranmer.

Chapter 7: Wyatt's Rebellion (1554)

Mary's heart was set on a marriage with a foreign prince, partly for reasons of prestige (why would she marry a subject?) and also because she wanted to reinvigorate England's position as a member of the wider Catholic, European Christendom. She was concerned, too, about the actions of France. The French heir was betrothed to the young Mary, Queen of Scots, who had a good claim to the English Crown – under common law, if Elizabeth were discounted on the grounds of illegitimacy, then the Queen of Scots would be Mary's heir.

After five centuries during which English history has perceived Spain as the enemy in the sixteenth century, it is hard to remember that, up until the reign of Elizabeth, Spain had been seen generally as an ally against the French and so, for Mary to look to Spain for alliance was not surprising, leaving aside that her own parents' marriage had been a manifestation of it.

Although initially Mary said she would have preferred an older man, she soon became persuaded that the most appropriate husband was Philip, twenty-seven years old and the son of her cousin, Emperor Charles V. Charles, although widowed, ruled himself out. He had been betrothed to Mary when she was just a child, and had supported her from a distance over many years, but tired, gouty and looking forward to abdicating, he put forward his son instead.

Mary was determined to have her way, despite misgivings among her Councillors – although none of them was so averse to the match that he couldn't be bought with a pension. Philip was heir to Spain, and the Low Countries, and the marriage treaty provided that any heir Mary bore would inherit England and the Low Countries - this would have been a huge benefit, had it come to pass, as Burgundy was England's biggest trading partner. Mary also made it clear that even after marriage, she would remain as sole monarch, and would not permit her husband to take any official part in government, although it is probable that most men doubted her on this.

A deputation from Parliament, tipped off by Gardiner, who supported a match with Courtenay, requested an audience from the Queen, in which they begged her not to marry a foreigner, lest he try to either take her abroad, or, in the event of her death, usurp the throne.

Mary was outraged by this interference with her royal prerogative and sent them off with a flea in their collective ear, taking Gardiner to task for putting them up to it. But she might have done better to listen. As soon as the proposed marriage became public knowledge, it stirred murmurings of discontent. Fear of foreigners was rife, and, amongst a vocal minority of Protestant gentry, this led to open rebellion, headed by

Sir Thomas Wyatt the Younger. Henry Grey, Duke of Suffolk, was also involved.

Wyatt claimed that his aim was just to prevent the match with Philip, but most people believed it was to replace Mary with either Jane Grey or Elizabeth, with the latter to be married to Courtenay. Courtenay himself was involved, but it was his revelation of the plot to his mentor, Gardiner, that enabled the Government to take preventative action to scotch part of the planned uprisings through the capture of Suffolk

Although isolated, Wyatt went ahead, and marched on London from Kent with a sizeable army. Mary, displaying her usual qualities of personal courage, iron determination and decisiveness in dangerous situations, reacted immediately. She called out her troops and, refusing to flee in the face of rebels heading for her capital, rode to the Guildhall and made an impassioned speech, defending her rights to the Crown and her determination to undertake the marriage only if it were of benefit to her people and consented to by Parliament. The rebels were defeated and Mary was safe.

Unfortunately, Jane Grey was not. Persuaded that as long as Jane lived, there would be uprisings in her favour, and also that Philip would not be arriving as long as there was any danger, the sentence of execution against Jane and her husband was carried out. Mary was clear that, if Jane accepted the Catholic faith she would be spared but Jane, just seventeen, would not renounce her faith.

Jane dispatched, the attention of many was diverted to Elizabeth. As before, Elizabeth had given no indication whatever of support for the rebels - but nor had she given much show of loyalty to Mary. There was evidence that potentially incriminated her - letters sent, that she denied receiving, and arrangements made for her to go to a particular house that, on being questioned, she denied remembering she even owned.

Elizabeth was sent to the Tower of London, whilst the evidence was examined.

Mary, although she had reluctantly accepted that Jane's death was necessary, was adamant that Elizabeth could not be convicted without solid proof. None was forthcoming, so, eventually, Elizabeth was sent from the Tower to house arrest at the old palace of Woodstock in Oxfordshire. Her guardian, Sir Henry Bedingfield, was the son of the man who had been Katharine of Aragon's guardian at Kimbolton Castle – presumably a deliberate choice. Nevertheless, Mary gave orders that, although Elizabeth was to be '*safeguarded*,' she was to be treated with the proper respect due to her position.

Meanwhile, Mary had achieved, on paper at least, one of her objectives. Parliament, chastened by the suppression of Wyatt's rebellion, and partially, if not wholly, reassured by the very favourable marriage treaty, ratified the Queen's marriage to Philip. It was reaffirmed that Mary was, and would remain, the only sovereign. It was also confirmed that England would not be expected to involve itself in Philip's Italian Wars, nor could Philip make any political appointments, whilst any power he held would be relinquished on her death. It was expected, however, that he would influence Mary, and, to an extent, he did.

Philip himself was not particularly eager for marriage to Mary. She was some eleven years older than him and he already had an heir from an earlier marriage (the mental health issues of his son, Don Carlos, were not yet apparent). Nevertheless, he was an obedient son, and in the summer of 1554, he sailed for England, armed with detailed advice as to how he should '*caress*' Mary's nobles and a warning that none of the soldiers on the fleet delivering him should be permitted to come ashore, lest it give weight to the French King's hints that Spain intended the conquest of England.

Philip arrived to a lavish, but rain-soaked, reception. Mary met her bridegroom privately two nights before the wedding. They talked for about an hour in front of the court – he speaking Spanish, she replying in French, although she taught him quickly to say goodnight to the company in English.

Mary and Philip were married at Winchester Cathedral on 25th July 1554, with the ceremony conducted by Gardiner, flanked by five other bishops. In order for Philip to have kingly rank, other than as Mary's husband, Charles had abdicated the Kingdom of Naples to him. Following the ceremony, they were proclaimed as Philip and Mary, Kings of England, France, Naples, Jerusalem, Ireland etc etc through a vast list of Princedoms, Archduchies and Lordships.

The royal couple returned to London, where, on the surface, the match was greeted with becoming rejoicing – pageants being prepared showing their union as a coming together of two descendants of Edward III, and portraying them as givers of justice and equality. Under the surface, however, anti-Spanish tensions ran high.

Chapter 8: Return to Rome

All appeared to be going swimmingly. In November 1554, it was agreed that Cardinal Pole would be readmitted to England. Pole had objected to Mary's marriage, and had also objected to her policy of proceeding slowly on the matter of the Papal Supremacy. Now, however, permitted to agree that former Church lands need not be returned, he returned to heal the schism of twenty years. In a huge ceremony at St Paul's, attended by some fifteen thousand people, Gardiner preached and the whole crowd knelt to receive Pole's blessing.

For Mary, who believed herself to be pregnant, this was probably the happiest moment of her life. There was much rejoicing as she retired to Hampton Court in spring of 1555, for the confinement. In her joy at the prospect of bearing an heir, Mary was reconciled with Elizabeth. Tragically, there was no pregnancy. The diagnosis is unsure - phantom pregnancy, ovarian cancer or some other disorder are all possible and for weeks Mary was subject to the intolerable humiliation of being told she had miscalculated the dates, whilst rumour spread, and her enemies sniggered behind their hands.

Soon after all hope had been relinquished, Philip left England for the Low Countries.

The Parliament of 1554 had reinstituted the heresy laws, repealed during Edward's reign. People convicted of heresy in the Church courts were to be handed over to the state for punishment, which might range from public penance, to a whipping, or for serious cases, death by burning.

Over the following three years 284 people were burnt. This is one of the most difficult aspects of Mary's reign to understand in the modern mind. In the sixteenth century, burning for heresy was considered an appropriate response as heretics endangered the souls of others, which was a terrible crime. Hanging, drawing, quartering, branding and having ears and hands chopped off were also normal punishments. The concept of freedom of conscience was almost unknown. Catholic and Protestant States all over Europe routinely slaughtered adherents of the wrong faith. Heretics and atheists had burnt under Henry VIII, under Edward VI and would continue to be cast into the flames in the reigns of Elizabeth and James I.

What is different in Mary's reign is, first, the scale of burnings (although they were a good deal less frequent than in Europe). In the past, heresy had been unusual and confined to a few people, but now, the Reformation had spread to the extent that there were vast numbers of people who believed differently. The burnings were carried out carefully, with due process of law, and only following attempts to persuade the heretic to recant. There was no mass hysteria or indiscriminate punishment. On each occasion, a member of the Queen's Council was present.

The second difference is political. History is written by the victors, and much of our knowledge of the persecutions has come from the radical Protestant, John Foxe's, 'Book of Acts and Monuments'. This work, written in the 1560s, became the most influential work in English after the Bible. It had a place on every Englishman's bookshelf and imbued a horror of popery that can still be recognised today.

The victims of the fires were drawn largely from the radical and vociferous proponents of their faith - people who kept quiet were not sought out. Mary's Government had a policy of encouraging radical Protestants to leave the country, and there was a steady stream of high-ranking exiles such as Katherine Willoughby, Dowager Duchess of Suffolk, and Sir Francis Knollys, married to Elizabeth's cousin, Katherine Carey, who took refuge in Geneva where Calvin had established his Protestant state. From there, a constant torrent of propaganda attacking Mary was launched.

Others, including Sir William Cecil, once Secretary to the Privy Council and an associate of both Somerset and Northumberland, conformed. He and his wife ostentatiously carried their rosaries and attended Mass. So long as a decent show of outward conformity was observed, no questions were asked as to inner thoughts, and many of the members of Mary's court were known to have been eager Protestants in the previous reign.

The unhappy effect of this was that many members of the court who conformed outwardly were not punished whilst the poor and defenceless were.

The most notable deaths were of the three bishops, Latimer, Ridley and Hooper, and, highest ranking of all, Thomas Cranmer, Archbishop of Canterbury. In a rare example of personal vindictiveness, the death of Cranmer was as certainly Mary's doing as if she had killed him with her own hand. In her mind, it was he who had destroyed her parents' marriage, and despite his recantation of Protestantism, he was not pardoned, as was the usual result, but sentenced to burn anyway. Stupidly, the authorities believed he would repeat his recantation on the face of the flames, but he did not, and pronounced his true beliefs for all to hear.

Despite most depictions of her, Mary's own religion was not the unregenerate superstition that the Humanists and Evangelicals had so derided in the 1520s. The programme that Pole and she planned to implement addressed many of the concerns of the early reformers. Priests were to be of good repute, live in their parishes, teach their flocks and live strictly according to their order. Education of the people in the practice of their religion was to be undertaken. Even a new translation of the Bible into English was planned. Mary gave generously to both Oxford and Cambridge, to improve training, and also, in a show of her personal tastes that was later maintained by Elizabeth, spent lavishly on the choirs and music of the Chapel Royal.

Many hard-line Catholics considered Cardinal Pole to be a heretic himself, as he was unsure in his own mind on the question of *'Justification by Faith Alone'* that had been the original point of divergence between those who sought to reform the Catholic Church, and those who considered its teachings to be wrong. Cardinal Pole's advice was to act as though good works were necessary, and to have faith as though it alone could justify a sinner. Whilst Mary's exact position on this doctrine is unknown, it is not unreasonable to assume that she and her Archbishop were in agreement. Where neither of them could tolerate any leanings towards Protestantism, was in the rejection of the doctrine of transubstantiation. This, effectively, became the test of whether a so-called heretic would burn or not.

This question of transubstantiation was a matter on which Mary's sister, and heir, Elizabeth could not be drawn (either then or later). Elizabeth was persuaded to attend Mass in the traditional form, but at the very moment when the priest performed the ritual that it was believed turned the bread into the body of Christ, she would suddenly have a stomach-ache or a coughing fit.

Chapter 9: Disappointment

The burnings continued, although it has been shown that they were reducing in numbers over the years as the most radical and vociferous Protestants were eliminated. This, together with the positive programme of Catholic education and reform, leads most modern scholars to believe that, had Mary's reign lasted longer, the old faith would have been sufficiently entrenched to remain the dominant faith in England. It is certainly not apparent from contemporary sources that the public at large saw the burnings as an unforgivable offence, although there were definite murmurings in London, which was the most Protestant area.

In late August 1555, Mary appeared in London with Philip, having emerged from the embarrassing months at Hampton Court. She was greeted with great enthusiasm by the crowd, which was no doubt a pleasing restorative, but two days later, she was obliged to watch as Philip departed for the Low Countries. Mary missed him badly, but consoled herself with the company of Pole, and also spent more time with Elizabeth, who went with her daily to Mass.

Mary's titles were augmented in late 1556 when Charles abdicated the Netherlands and the throne of Spain to Philip. In return, Philip wanted to be crowned as King of England and gave Mary to understand that that might be the price of his return. He also suggested that she might like to join in his war with France.

Well aware that neither of these courses would be acceptable to her subjects, Mary was obliged to resist Philip's requests.

The disappointment of the phantom pregnancy, the departure of Philip, and the depressing sight of martyrs burning, was exacerbated by the economic problems of the mid-1550s. There were several years of appalling harvests, which combined with inflation and the straitened circumstances of the Crown to create an air of gloom.

New coinage was issued to try to get on top of the inflation caused by debasement, and a good deal of retrenchment and even penny pinching began, but Crown finances, which had never recovered from Henry VIII's expenditure, and the poor husbandry of Edward's protectors, were not helped by Mary's insistence on returning many of the former monastic lands held by the Crown to the Church.

In early 1556 a new plot was discovered. Led by Sir Henry Dudley, cousin of the late Duke of Northumberland, and other Protestants, who had previously been associated with Sir Thomas Wyatt, it had been partially financed and wholly encouraged by the King of France.

Cardinal Pole was informed of the plot by an Exchequer official who became aware that part of the plan was to steal the bullion from the Tower. The ringleaders, with the exception of Dudley, who had escaped to France, were executed. Elizabeth's household also fell under suspicion – her Governess, Kat Ashley, was found to have incriminating literature, but Elizabeth herself was not accused of involvement. With Mary childless, the alternative heir to Elizabeth was Mary, Queen of Scots, who would one day be Queen of France. Such a state of affairs was the last thing Philip wanted, so he discouraged Mary from proceeding against her sister.

In return for his protection, Philip wanted Elizabeth to marry his ally, Emmanuel Philibert of Savoy. Mary was distinctly unimpressed with this plan – partly because Elizabeth had rejected the idea out of hand and Mary was reluctant to coerce her, although she threatened to have Elizabeth publicly disinherited and replaced with Mary, Queen of Scots. Mary might also have been chary of giving Elizabeth wider European support.

She wrote to Philip that there was no prospect of the marriage being agreed without him returning to England, so in March 1557 he came back. Top of his agenda was persuading Mary to join the war against France. Bizarrely, this war led to Philip being in direct conflict with the Pope, who, in retaliation, tried to recall Cardinal Pole to Rome to face heresy charges.

Mary might have believed in Papal Supremacy, but she would no more let the Pope dictate to her than any of her predecessors would. She categorically refused to let Pole leave the country and be replaced with a Papal nominee. She informed the Pope that, if there were any charges of heresy to be preferred against Pole, that they must be heard in England, and in any event, she took him for a good Catholic.

Whilst there seems little to choose between France and Spain in the matter of the ongoing war between them, it was undeniable that France had actively sought to undermine Mary, supporting plots against her, and harbouring traitors. Although Henri II did not wish to be in a state of open war with England, Mary had had enough of his interference. Two new ships had been commissioned – the *Philip and Mary*, and a new *Mary Rose* and they were ready for war by early 1557. Additionally, 6000 foot and 600 horse were raised.

Mary summoned her Council, and on 1st April, requested them to approve a declaration of war against France. After two days of deliberation, they rejected her request. Whilst they would support Philip with money and ships, in accordance with the marriage treaty, England should go no further. Open war with France would be economically disastrous. Mary was incandescent with rage, and, taking them one by one, bullied them into offering troops, although an open declaration of war was still resisted.

Mary and Philip were not satisfied, and then the French again provoked hostility by funding a ludicrous invasion by Sir Thomas Stafford (a nephew of Cardinal Pole, but a Protestant). He landed in Scarborough, whose castle he seized. Quickly captured and executed, he had furnished the casus belli needed for a declaration of war on France. Henri received it derisively, saying he could not even be bothered to listen to such a challenge from a woman.

Philip departed on 6th July. Despite the misgivings of the Council, the nobility, who hadn't had a chance to show off in armour since 1543, were all agog to join the King in his expedition. A force of over 1,000, led by William Herbert, Earl of Pembroke (and a Protestant) joined the King. It included the sons of the late Duke of Northumberland and other young men eager to claim glory in a foreign war. The combined Anglo-Spanish troops won a resounding victory at St Quentin but Philip, always cautious, did not follow up with an attack on Paris.

Unfortunately, one of the areas where Government expenditure had been slashed was in the defence of Calais. Calais was the last English toehold in France and thus was hugely symbolic, even if it was a practical nuisance and drain on resources. The Governor, Thomas, Baron Wentworth, had warned of decaying defences, but no money was available for repairs.

Whilst Philip was dithering about his next move, a lightening swoop by Henri II and the Duke of Guise (uncle of Mary, Queen of Scots) recaptured Calais on 7th January, 1558. The outlying fortresses of Guisnes and Hammes held out for another two weeks, but had no choice by 21st January but surrender.

Mary, her Government, her Parliament and her people were appalled, but there was no money or leadership to take it back. Philip, having achieved his objectives hadn't the slightest interest in recapturing the town. She is alleged to have mourned this bitter climax to her reign with the words 'When I am dead and opened, you shall find Calais engraved on my heart.'

Adding to her grief, were both the dashing of her revived hopes of pregnancy, and the ongoing wrangle with Pope Paul IV over Cardinal Pole. Although a truce had been signed in September between Philip and the Pope, Pole had not been officially reinstated as Papal Legate, and Mary's relationship with the papacy continued to be strained. She repeatedly reaffirmed her obedience to the Holy See, but nevertheless, she would not hand Pole over or accept any other Papal nominees.

These repeated blows of fortune drove Mary into increasingly poor health and, perhaps, depression. Although she had implied that she would name the Catholic Lady Margaret Douglas, Countess of Lennox as her heir, the reality was that Elizabeth was next in line. Mary tried to persuade Elizabeth to confirm her adherence to the Catholic faith, but Elizabeth equivocated. Nevertheless, Mary would not take the step of forcing her sister to marry, as Philip had previously suggested, which would have taken her out of the country.

Chapter 10: The End of an Era

In the summer and autumn of 1558, after another poor harvest, a severe epidemic of influenza struck England. People died in their thousands and the Queen fell ill. She had made her Will in hope of bearing a child, but, knowing that was now impossible, she added a codicil, not specifically naming Elizabeth, but referring to her heir *'by the Laws and Statutes of the Realm'*. She directed that her father's and brother's debts be paid, and left bequests for the new religious houses she created. She also wanted her mother's body to be exhumed and laid to rest with her. None of these wishes was carried out.

At the very end, Mary accepted that Elizabeth must follow her, and sent her the coronation ring. Mary died, aged 42, at St James' Palace. Her funeral oration was preached by John White, Bishop of Winchester who praised her in glowing terms:

'.she used singular mercy towards offenders. She used much pity and compassion towards the poor and oppressed...I verily believe, the poorest creature in all this city feared not God more than she did.'

Elizabeth was not amused and had the bishop thrown into gaol.

Mary left a terrible memory of religious persecution, much of which was created by propaganda long after her reign, but she also proved that a woman could rule as well as a man, and that a Queen of England had the same power, majesty and authority as any King. Her tomb is at Westminster Abbey, where she lies interred with Elizabeth under the words (in Latin)

'Partners both in throne and grave, here rest we two sisters, Mary and Elizabeth, in the hope of one resurrection.'

Part 2: Aspects of Mary I's Life

Chapter 11: A Controversial Marriage

One of the decisions that Mary made which was controversial both at the time, and subsequently, was her marriage. Hindsight is a useful tool, but not one which Mary had the advantage of possessing. Would looking at the matter without knowing the outcome, give a different view of her choices?

There are three elements that should be considered in analysing Mary's marriage: her decision to marry at all; the choice of spouse; and whether it achieved her objectives.

Should the Queen Marry?

In the sixteenth century, and indeed for many centuries afterward, a deliberate decision to remain unmarried was outside the paradigm of how people perceived the individual and society. It was every person's duty to marry. Amongst poorer people, marriage was necessary because a single person was not generally a functioning economic unit. Higher up the social scale, marriages were about creating political and economic alliances between families and passing on wealth. Failure to have an heir might mean the families' lands would revert to the Crown.

Amongst Kings, marriage was for creating alliances between countries, and for providing an heir, ideally male. It was the very fear over the absence of a male heir that goaded Mary's father into the annulment of his marriage to Mary's mother. Mary herself had been betrothed several times during her father's lifetime – it was his concern that a husband might take it upon himself to back Mary's claim to the throne with force, or undermine the position of Edward, that kept Mary single before she became queen.

With this in mind, the assumption that not only Mary, but also all of her advisors, except one, made in 1553, was that she should marry. Mary expressed some personal reservations, hardly surprising in a woman who was, presumably, a virgin, and perhaps nervous of the physical side of marriage (although we should not think of Tudor women as Victorian ladies, terrified of sex). Perhaps mindful of the debacle of Anne of Cleves, Mary hoped that she would be able to meet her prospective bridegroom before committing herself, but this was not really a practical proposition.

The sole exception to the assumption about marriage was her cousin, Cardinal Reginald Pole, presumably on account of Mary's age. At thirty-seven and not in robust health, her chances of bearing an heir were rapidly diminishing, and if she had become pregnant, the risk of her dying in childbed was high. Compared with this risk, considering her parents and grandparents, Mary might have been expected to reach her mid-fifties.

Any King would also have been expected to marry. The complication arose because Mary's advisors, and to a degree the Queen herself, anticipated that a husband would have more influence over his wife and in Government, than a Queen-Consort would have had. It would also have been anticipated that, if Mary died bearing a living child, her husband would have expected a role in a Regency government. In England, there was no history of Queens Consort as Regents for their children, although it was not uncommon in other European countries, including Scotland. Thus the choice of a husband for Mary had more political weight than the choice of a Queen Consort might have had.

The fact that Mary's half-sister, Elizabeth, was continually pressed to marry, well into the 1580s suggests that no-one questioned Mary's decision to marry in principle. It is only with the benefit of hindsight that we can say Elizabeth's decision not to, was sound – although we do not know what would have happened if Elizabeth had married – it might have turned out well.

Whom should the Queen Marry?

A husband could be chosen either from the nobility of England, or from a European prince. Marriage to a subject had occurred in 1464, with the wedding of Edward IV and Elizabeth Woodville, and, of course, between Henry VIII and four of his wives, but such marriages were unknown outside England, and had not generally proved that popular in the country. Certainly Edward IV's marriage had caused huge resentment. If Edward IV's relatives and advisors had been horrified at the promotion of a subject, and the rewards and preferment that Elizabeth Woodville's family received, how much more would a marriage to a man who would then, in the eyes of the nobles, become King, have been resented?

In any event, there were few home-grown choices who were remotely possible. The only males with royal blood were Edward Courtenay, the great-grandson of Edward IV; Reginald Pole, great-nephew of Edward IV; Henry and George Hastings, 3x great-nephews of Edward IV; and Henry Stuart, Lord Darnley, grandson of Margaret Tudor, Queen of Scots.

Lord Darnley and George Hastings were both around thirteen so completely unsuitable and Henry Hastings was married – to the daughter of the Duke of Northumberland. That left Courtenay, aged twenty-six and Pole.

Courtenay had been sent to the Tower of London at the age of eleven, following the Exeter Conspiracy, which resulted in the execution of his father, Henry Courtenay, Marquess of Exeter. He had only been released on Mary's accession.

Courtenay was favoured by a significant group of Mary's Council, including her Lord Chancellor, Stephen Gardiner, who had become fond of the young man when both were in the Tower during Edward's reign. Courtenay's suit was also promoted by his mother, Gertrude Blount, one of Mary's closest friends and by many of the men who had been her most faithful supporters during Edward's reign.

Mary, however, considered him completely unsuitable – he was too young, a subject with no lands or power of his own, and was, not surprisingly given his long-term incarceration, immature and lacking in judgement. When pressed, Mary snapped at her Chancellor that his friendship for the man was not a good reason for her to marry a subject. It is not hard to imagine that a marriage to Courtenay might well have created the problems later caused by the marriage of Mary's cousin, the Queen of Scots to the aforementioned Lord Darnley, who had some of the same characteristics.

Reginald Pole had been suggested as a husband for Mary some seventeen years before, by the rebels of the Pilgrimage of Grace, much to her father's chagrin. He had been in exile since the early 1530s, and although not an ordained priest in 1553, he was a Cardinal and a scholar. He was also still a subject of the Queen, and had nothing to bring to a marriage, other than his Plantagenet blood. In any event, Mary had other ideas for his future – leadership of the Church in England.

That left a foreign match. But whom could she choose? The French King, Henri II, to whom she had once been betrothed, was already married, and his sons were children – the oldest, only nine, was also contracted to Mary, Queen of Scots. There was Erik, the Prince of Sweden, only twenty, and a Lutheran, so not a good prospect. Another potential candidate was Dom Luis of Portugal, who had been suggested as a spouse for Mary several times in the past. He was her first cousin, and ten years her senior. He might have proved a good choice – not a King at home, so more able to spend time in England and old enough, presumably, to have maturity and judgement.

There were also Ferdinand of Austria (later Holy Roman Emperor) another cousin, who had been widowed since 1548 and Ferdinand's son of the same name who was unmarried and of suitable age. As the elder Ferdinand had more than enough children (thirteen who lived to adulthood) and was constantly occupied in war with the Sultan of Turkey, and helping his brother, Emperor Charles V, with maintaining Hapsburg dominance, he would have had little incentive to marry again. His second son, although only 24, was a definite possibility, and Ferdinand senior wrote to Charles requesting the latter to stop trying to prevent the match.

There was the widowed Emperor Charles himself, and his widowed son, Philip. Mary would originally have preferred the father – she had fond childhood memories of Charles and believed that he had supported her throughout her life. With the benefit of the availability of his correspondence with his ambassadors which Mary never saw, we can see that his support of Mary was qualified, and never allowed to interfere with his own duties or ambitions, but for her, it had been a life-line.

Charles wanted Mary to marry Philip, and given that Mary believed that Charles had always had her best interests at heart, she was willing to accept his advice. Philip himself was distinctly unenthusiastic, although he accepted his father's decision obediently. He had a long-term mistress, and was negotiating for a marriage with yet another cousin, an Infanta of Portugal, like his first wife.

Historically, friendship, if not formal alliance, with the Low Countries had been a plank of English Kings' foreign policy. The Low Countries were England's biggest trading partner and any breach was economically disastrous. Castile, too, had been an ally for centuries, providing a Queen for Edward I, and a King as husband for John of Gaunt's daughter, Katherine of Lancaster. Alliance with the countries of the Iberian peninsula was considered an important tool in the on-going pursuit of the French Crown. The Spanish alliance represented by the marriage of Katharine of Aragon, first to Arthur, Prince of Wales, and then to Henry VIII, had been widely popular. Considering this history, Mary's policy of marrying Philip, who was not just King of Spain but also the ruler of the Low Countries, seemed to be an obvious decision.

Unfortunately, public perceptions of this foundered again on the rock of Mary's gender. It is impossible to imagine that, had Edward VI lived and chosen to marry a Spanish princess, anyone would have dreamed of questioning his choice. It was the assumption that Philip would not just be Mary's consort, but that he would become King and subject England to Spanish rule that worried people.

Times had changed, too, since the marriage of Henry and Katharine. The concept of the nation-state was beginning to form. The development of the Reformation and growing populations across Europe were creating a much stronger perception of nations as fixed entities, rather than fluid inheritances of kings. The English had always been hostile to 'foreigners'

– there are numerous mediaeval reports of riots against perceived interlopers in London, and whilst creating international alliances was clearly the job of the monarch, the fear of domination was real and the heavy-handed rule of Charles and Philip in the Low Countries caused unease. It was this marriage that was the criticism most widely made of Mary during her life-time, and during Elizabeth's reign, when Spain came to be seen as the enemy.

Mary's Council was divided. Gardiner, in particular, urged her to marry Courtenay, then the Commons, led by Speaker Sir John Pollock, brought a petition to her, to marry, but not to a foreigner.

Mary reacted with all the fury of a thwarted Tudor, not even following etiquette by allowing Gardiner to reply for her. She leapt to her feet, having been obliged to sit by the lengthiness of Pollock's address and began. She was very grateful, of course, to Parliament for its advice to marry but she thought their second point *very strange*.

'Parliament,' she said, *'was not accustomed to use such language to the Kings of England, nor was it suitable or respectful that they should do so.'* Even Kings in their minority had not been interfered with in the matter of marriage. Having made her point that she would brook no interference in her choice of husband, Mary then caressed them with words of love, assuring them she thought of nothing but the welfare of the kingdom as a good *'princess and mistress'* should do. This was certainly true – the question was whether she was right in her interpretation of the good of the realm.

Not everyone was convinced that Mary's decision to marry a Spaniard was the right one, and rebellion followed – certainly fomented by Henri II of France, who was nervous of any alliance between England and Spain, but with fairly widespread support for the fundamental point that Mary should not marry Philip.

The Tudors were not the seventeenth century Stuarts – they knew very well, in practical terms, that they ruled by the consent of the people, rather than by Divine Right, but they would resist encroachment on their prerogatives to the utmost, before they would pretend to give in, with a show of charm and love, prior to doing exactly what they wanted. It was a trick that Henry VIII had used with the Pilgrimage of Grace, and that Elizabeth would use frequently.

Mary, too, knew all about courting public opinion and, whilst her Council were urging her to flee London in the face of the oncoming rebels, led by Sir Thomas Wyatt the Younger (son of the poet), she rode into London to make a speech at the Guildhall. In it, she promised that whilst she was convinced of the merits of the proposed match, she would not continue with it without Parliament's consent. Even those who were opposed to her policies, admitted that Mary's speech carried the crowd and she departed in triumph.

Wyatt dispatched, Parliament accepted the treaty as drafted – in every respect, it was favourable to England. Philip had no sovereign power, or right to make political appointments, could not involve England in the Hapsburg-Valois wars, could not take Mary out of the country, and any child was to inherit both England and the Low Countries, which would have been a great gain. Nevertheless, Mary was the only one who was really pleased with the deal struck.

Did the Marriage Achieve Mary's Objectives?

On 25th July 1554, Mary was married at Winchester Cathedral. She was attended by her cousins, Lady Margaret Douglas, Countess of Lennox, and Lady Katherine Grey, both potential heirs to the throne. Elizabeth, suspected of involvement in the Wyatt rebellion was under house arrest.

Philip had arrived a couple of days before and made great efforts throughout the time he spent in England to be pleasant and obliging and to court public approval. He treated Mary respectfully and courteously, and if he found his marital duty hard, which some of his friends suspected, he did not let her know. They spent a good deal of time together, and had interests in common, particularly music.

Philip did not have Mary's facility with languages. He understood French, but does not seem to have spoken it, so they conversed with him speaking Spanish, and she replying in French and some Spanish or Italian, although she also taught him a few English phrases. Nevertheless, although it seems that Mary became deeply attached to Philip, he did not return her love – perhaps not surprising given their relative ages and different upbringings.

As much as any personal qualities Philip may have had, it was probably a great relief to Mary to have an adult with whom she could have a relationship of equality, something that she had not had since the death of Katherine Parr, and the first time she had had such a relationship with a man.

But personal happiness was not the object of royal marriage. The main purpose was the begetting of an heir, and in this it failed. Mary thought she was pregnant in 1555, as did all her doctors and attendants, but it became apparent that the pregnancy was false. A repeat of the symptoms of whatever the underlying cause was, gave Mary hope in early 1558, but again, proved to be an illusion.

The second objective Mary had was a reintegration of England into Catholic Christendom. When her marriage was first negotiated, Henri II of France had suggested that it would end in hostility between France and England. Mary assured him that she intended to keep on good terms with France, but, in the end, Henri was proved right – although his policy of supporting her rebels was hardly conducive to peace. The combination of Henri's provocations and Philip's on-going Italian Wars resulted in Mary forcing her Council to support a declaration of war.

Despite initial success, the loss of Calais overshadowed the last year of Mary's reign, and her subsequent reputation. Finally, the rivalry between the Hapsburgs and Pope Paul IV in Italy isolated Mary even from the positive relationship with the Holy See that she had hoped to establish.

In summary, it does appear that, although the decision Mary made can be defended on the basis of the information she had, the results were very different from what she had hoped.

Chapter 12: Following the Footsteps of Mary I

Like many English monarchs, Mary spent the majority of her time in the palaces surrounding London, but she also spent time in the Welsh Marches, and, during her brother's reign, significant amounts of time in East Anglia, the heart of the great landed estate she came into possession of in 1547.

The numbers in the article below correspond to those on the map which follows.

*

Mary was born at the Palace of Placentia, in Greenwich (1). The palace had originally been built by Humphrey, Duke of Gloucester, brother of Henry V in 1443: forfeit to the Crown when the Duke died, the palace proved popular with all subsequent monarchs. Mary was christened in the Church of the Observant Friars, next to the palace. Greenwich, as it was generally known, continued to be used by the Tudor monarchs, and also by James VI & I and Charles I. It was demolished on the Restoration of Charles II, and the Royal Naval College built on the site.

During her childhood, Mary travelled around the palaces and royal manors and castles that surrounded London, sometimes with her parents, sometimes with just her own attendants. In 1525, aged nine, she was sent to Ludlow (2), in the Marches of Wales, to preside over the Council of Wales and the Marches. Ludlow had been part of the Mortimer inheritance of Richard, Duke of York, and was subsumed into the Crown when Edward IV became king. Although Mary was not formally invested as Princess of Wales, her regime there was similar to that of her great-uncle, Edward V, and her father's older brother, Prince Arthur.

Mary and her Council remained based at Ludlow for the following three years, with visits to other properties in the region, notably Tickenhill (sometimes referred to as Bewdley or Beaulieu after the town near Kidderminster in which it was situated). It was at Tickenhill that Mary's uncle Arthur had been married by proxy to her mother, Katharine of Aragon in 1499. Like Ludlow, Tickenhill (3) was part of the lands of the Mortimers and was enhanced and extended by Edward IV. It consisted of a timber palace with a great hall of at least 100 feet in length, outhouses, a chapel, gardens and a gatehouse. It was replaced in the eighteenth century by the privately owned manor house which still stands.

Another of the great houses Mary occupied during her sojourn in Wales was the castle of Thornbury (4). Thornbury was a very modern building in the 1520s. Construction had begun in 1511 under Edward

Stafford, 3rd Duke of Buckingham. Visiting Thornbury must have been a bitter pill for Mary's Governess, Lady Salisbury, whose daughter, Ursula, was married to Buckingham's oldest son. Instead of seeing her daughter as chatelaine, Lady Salisbury was forced to remember that the pride and royal pretensions of Buckingham that had created the grandeur of Thornbury, had resulted in his execution for treason in 1521. His possessions were all forfeit to the Crown. Today, Thornbury is a luxury hotel. Much of the original Tudor building still stands, and it is well worth a visit, although you may have to save up to stay in one of the sumptuous rooms!

Once Mary was recalled from Wales permanently in 1528, she again spent most of her time near London. One of the houses she resided in frequently, right up until her accession as Queen in 1553, was the manor of Hunsdon (5), in Hertfordshire. It was built in the mid-sixteenth century by the Yorkist Sir William Oldhall. Oldhall's son, John, fell at Bosworth and his lands were forfeit to the Crown, although later granted for life to Thomas Howard, 2nd Duke of Norfolk, presumably to show royal gratitude after Norfolk's victory at Flodden. It reverted to the Crown in 1524 and Henry VIII expanded it significantly. Edward and Elizabeth also lived at Hunsdon, and one of the portraits of Edward shows the house in the background.

On Elizabeth's accession, she granted it to her cousin, Henry Carey, later Baron Hunsdon. The present building, extensively remodelled and reduced in size from the original, is in private hands. The adjoining church shows many Tudor features, and Mary is known to have acted as godmother to at least one local child.

Another palace associated with Mary's youth is Hatfield (6), also in Hertfordshire, although for Mary, her time there was deeply unhappy. It was to Hatfield that she was sent to act as attendant to the baby

Elizabeth, who had supplanted her. The original red-brick palace was built by John Morton, Bishop of Ely and later Cardinal-Archbishop of Canterbury, who was one of the most dedicated supporters of Henry VII.

Morton's palace, in a traditional square formation, was built around 1497. It was at Hatfield that Elizabeth heard of the death of Mary, and received the coronation ring from her sister's hand. Only one wing of this is left, the remainder having been pulled down and the bricks used to create the fantastic Hatfield House of Robert Cecil, Earl of Salisbury. Salisbury's house remains, set in wonderful parklands and gardens, and is open to the public.

Mary also spent time at Hertford Castle (7) – it was to Hertford that she was sent when Queen Katheryn Howard's household was disbanded. She was ordered to join Prince Edward there. Hertford, originally constructed by Henry II, was granted to John of Gaunt, Duke of Lancaster, and became a favoured home of the Lancastrian Kings and their wives, Catherine de Valois and Marguerite of Anjou. It was then granted by Edward IV to his wife, Elizabeth Woodville, but Richard III deprived her of it and gave it to Henry Stafford, Duke of Buckingham.

Confiscated following Buckingham's rebellion, it was given to Elizabeth of York when Henry VII took the throne. Henry VIII extended the castle and built the gatehouse. Mary received the castle during Edward's reign and spent considerable periods of time there. Hertford, too, became part of the lands of the Cecil Earls of Salisbury until it was given to Hertford Town Council. The gatehouse houses the Council's offices and the grounds may be visited by the public.

In Henry VIII's will, Mary was bequeathed income, but not land. This changed when the Regency Council, which interpreted Henry's will very liberally, made huge land grants to its members. Mary and Elizabeth were both included in the giveaway, although Mary received by far the greatest share. As part of her holdings, she was given both the manor of Kenninghall, and the castle of Framlingham. Both of these properties, in Norfolk and Suffolk respectively, had been confiscated from Thomas Howard, 3rd Duke of Norfolk, following his attainder for treason. Kenninghall, an ancient manor, had been rebuilt during the period 1505-1525 and was a grand Tudor construction, with an H-plan layout and 700 acres of parkland.

Kenninghall (8) appears to have been one of Mary's favourite residences during the period 1547 – 1553. It was to Kenninghall that she first rode when she heard of the death of Edward VI, to raise her affinity and resist the coup aimed at depriving her of her Crown. En route, she stopped at Sawston Hall (9) in Cambridgeshire, home of the Huddleston family. The old Sawston Hall was burnt to the ground by Northumberland's men, within hours of her departure, but she paid for a replacement, which remained in the family until 1982. It is still in private hands, little changed since the 1550s, except for the addition of three priest-holes during Elizabeth's reign.

With the high number of men joining her, and the need to have a stout castle, capable of defence should Northumberland bring an army against her, Mary moved from Kenninghall to Framlingham (10). Originally a Norman keep, it belonged to successive Earls and Dukes of Norfolk, until it was forfeited in 1547 and granted to Mary. During the previous decades, it had been extended with pleasure gardens and comfortable internal chambers. The nearby St Mary's Church became a mausoleum for the Howard family, following the Dissolution of Thetford Priory.

In 1553, Mary restored both Kenninghall and Framlingham to the Duke of Norfolk, but they were forfeited again when the 4th Duke, Thomas, lost his head for plotting to marry Mary, Queen of Scots. The castle was used in the later sixteenth century as a prison for Catholic recusants. It is now in the care of English Heritage, and makes a fine day out for families.

On 1st October, Mary was crowned at Westminster Abbey (11) as the majority of her forbears had been since 1066. She was crowned with the same ceremony and accoutrements as a King, with the exception of also being given the consort's sceptre to hold in her left hand, and not donning the spurs of knighthood, although she was belted with the sword.

Six months after her coronation, Mary was again called upon to defend her throne in the face of Sir Thomas Wyatt's rebels. Whilst the rebels were encamped on the south side of the Thames, Mary rode to the Guildhall (12) in London, where she made a rousing speech, scorning to show weakness in the face of threats. The Londoners, who by and large, were probably as anti the proposed Spanish match as Wyatt, were impressed by their Queen and, cheering her wildly, defended the city against Wyatt's men. The Guildhall today is still used for functions for the Corporation of London, most notably, the annual Lord Mayor's Dinner. There is also an art gallery with a surprisingly wide range of work.

Having shown her power, Mary proceeded with the planned marriage, which took place at Winchester Cathedral (13) on 25th July, 1554. The date was St James' Day, presumably picked to honour the Patron Saint of Spain. Mary arrived in Winchester some days before the wedding and stayed in the Bishop's Palace. After the ceremony, the royal couple spent around ten days in the city. Today, Winchester Cathedral, which has the longest nave in Europe, houses the tomb of the celebrated author Jane Austen.

By the beginning of the following year, Mary believed herself to be pregnant and withdrew to Hampton Court (14) for the birth of an heir. Sadly, her physical symptoms were not those of pregnancy, and, after months of agonising doubt and humiliation, she left Hampton Court to have a brief period of respite at Oatlands Palace. Hampton Court is, of course, one of the great Tudor palaces still open to visitors, even though much of the original was replaced 150 years after Mary's time by her name-sake, Queen Mary II, and King William III.

Mary's health was never robust, and by the autumn of 1558 she was gravely ill with the influenza that had carried off thousands of her subjects. She died at St James's Palace, (15) London. St James's was built in the early 1530s on the site of a former leper hospital and the Tudor gatehouse flanks the south side of Pall Mall. It remains the official residence of the Sovereign – ambassadors are credited to '*the Court of St James*'. No monarch has resided there since 1837, however, several other members of the Royal Family have apartments there, although the Tudor and Stuart royal apartments were destroyed by fire in the nineteenth century. The Queen's Chapel, designed by Inigo Jones, is sometimes open to the public.

Mary's heart was interred in the Chapel Royal at St James's, but her body was buried in Westminster Abbey, in the Lady Chapel founded by her grandfather, Henry VII. She lies there still. In her will, she requested that her mother be laid beside her, and that the two of them should be given an '*honourable tomb or memorial*' for a '*decent memory*' of the both. Neither of these wishes was carried out and Mary has no monument. The effigy above her grave is that of her half-sister, Elizabeth, who was moved there from her original location to make room for James VI & I.

The list below corresponds to the map which follows of places Mary would have known.

Key to Map

1. Greenwich Palace, Greater London
2. Ludlow Castle, Shropshire
3. Tickenhill Palace, Worcestershire
4. Thornbury Castle, Gloucestershire
5. Hunsdon Manor, Hertfordshire
6. Hatfield Palace, Hertfordshire
7. Hertford Castle, Hertfordshire
8. Kenninghall Manor, Norfolk
9. Sawston Hall, Cambridgeshire
10. Framlingham Castle, Suffolk
11. Westminster Abbey, London
12. Guildhall, London
13. Winchester Cathedral, Hampshire
14. Hampton Court Palace, Surrey
15. St James' Palace, London

Map

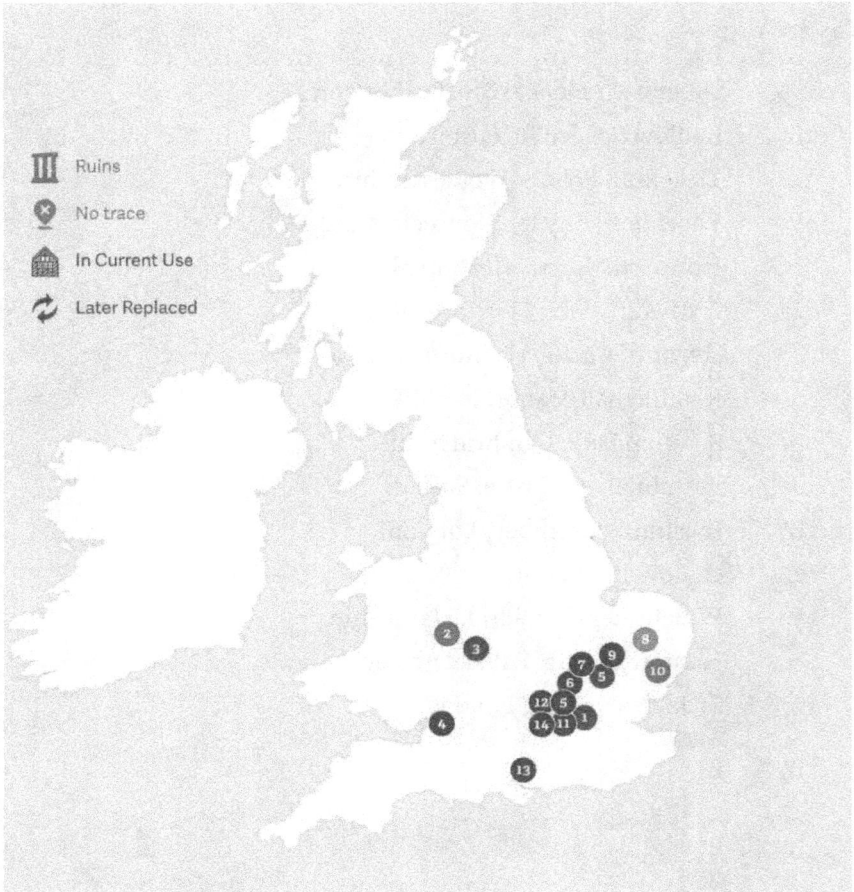

Chapter 13: The Mary Tudor Pearl

Pictures of Mary after she became Queen show her wearing a large pearl, suspended from the jewelled ornament pinned to the centre of her bodice. At one time, it was believed that this was the pearl later known as *La Peregrina* ('the Pilgrim'), one of the largest pearls ever found. *La Peregrina* was owned by the actress, Elizabeth Taylor, but was actually smaller than Mary's which has been shown by recent research to be a different gem.

At 64.5 carats and 258.12 grams, Mary's is the third largest natural pearl known. If the diamond tip is included, it is a stunning 69.8 carats!

According to the most up-to-date information, Mary's pearl was found in around 1526, and became part of the jewellery collection of Isabella of Portugal – the mutual cousin for whom the Emperor Charles V jilted Mary. Empress Isabella died in 1539, leaving the gem to her daughter, Juana of Austria.

Juana married her double cousin, Prince Joao Manuel of Portugal, but returned to Spain on his death in 1554. The pearl was then sent to Mary I as part of the negotiations for her marriage to Juana's brother, Philip of Spain.

It has always been assumed that it was returned to Spain on Mary's death, but in her will, although she specifies other gems he gave her, including large table diamonds, she does not specify the pearl.

It may be that, as the two gems are linked in the pendant Mary wore, she considered it a single item, although that would not be my first interpretation of her bequest:

'[to my husband] to keep for a memory of me one jewel, being a table diamond, which the Emperor's Majesty…sent unto me by the Count d'Egmont at the insurance [presumably 'request'] of my said Lord and Husband and also the other table diamond which His Majesty sent unto me…and the collar of gold, set with nine diamond… and also the ruby set in a gold ring.'

The pearl has been assumed to be that which was then named in an inventory of jewels made in 1574 on the death of Juana of Austria. Unsold in the ensuing auction, it was eventually purchased in 1581 by a silversmith, Diego Ruiz for 3,300 reales. It then disappeared from view until 2004, when it was purchased for £155,000. It is owned by Symbolic & Chase.

Chapter 14: Mary I in Fact and Fiction

Portrayals of Mary I have been almost overwhelmingly negative, beginning with John Knox and his *First Blast of the Trumpet against the Monstrous Regiment of Women* and John Foxe's *Book of Acts and Monuments*. More nuanced portraits appeared in the later nineteenth and early twentieth centuries.

Mary in Fact

We are aware of five major modern biographies of Mary:

Mary Tudor, by David Loades. David Loades is a widely respected historian with a distinguished academic pedigree who has written extensively about the Tudor period. His book on Mary, first published in the 1989, but updated in 2011, was the first modern biography of the Queen. Personally, I find Professor Loades has moved very little from the perception of Mary as an hysterical woman, totally dominated by her husband, whose failed reign was just a prologue to the glories of Elizabeth.

Mary Tudor: England's First Queen, by Anna Whitelock. Dr Whitelock's central thesis is that Mary's reign, although short, demonstrated that a Queen-regnant could wield power in exactly the same fashion as a King. Mary did not necessarily always use that power wisely – the pressure put on the Council to agree to the war in France perhaps being an example – but in that she was no different from any other monarch. Mary made female power, if not welcome to her male contemporaries, at least respected and accepted.

The Myth of Bloody Mary: A biography of Queen Mary I of England, by Linda Porter. Dr Porter's biography is a well-rounded and sympathetic portrayal of Mary, although it perhaps minimises Mary's role in the religious persecution to a degree that is inconsistent with Porter's overall analysis of Mary as a woman in control of events.

Mary I: England's Catholic Queen, by John Edwards. This biography is from the highly-reputable, scholarly, Yale stable. Edwards makes extensive use of Spanish sources, providing a different and interesting angle to his work, which is detailed and engrossing.

Mary Tudor, by Judith M Richards. Published by Routledge, this too is a scholarly, rather than a popular biography, and introduces much of the new thinking on Mary's Catholicism as closer to Evangelical and Counter-Reformation ideals, rather than traditional mediaeval piety.

*

Two volumes of essays looking either at aspects of her life or comparing her approach to specific issues with that of Elizabeth have recently been published.   Fascinating though they are, it raises the question of why must Mary always be compared with Elizabeth?   There are not many examples of historical accounts that compare other monarchs with his or her successor, even a sibling – how common are joint biographies of Richard I and King John; Edward IV and Richard III; Mary II and Anne; George IV and William IV?

Tudor Queenship: The Reigns of Mary and Elizabeth (Queenship and Power), ed Anna Whitelock & Alice Hunt. This is a fascinating series of essays by a wide range of experts looking at different aspects of the lives and reigns of the half-sisters, sometimes drawing immediate comparisons, but often illuminating previously unremarked elements of the life of one or other.

Mary Tudor: Old and New Perspectives, ed Susan Doran and Thomas. S. Freeman. This is another collection of informative essays, which contrasts accounts, both favourable and inimical, from the 16th to 20th centuries, and the new, more nuanced interpretations of the last twenty years.

In addition, there is the work of ***Professor Eamonn Duffy***, whose ***Fires of Faith*** has done much to challenge received opinion on the religious persecutions of the reign although critics sometimes find it too much of a whitewash and not much less biased than the Protestant polemics.

*

Mary also appears in group biographies. The analysis of her life and reign in the hugely influential ***Lives of the Queens of England*** by

Agnes Strickland created a furore at the time, as it challenged perceptions of Mary as bloodthirsty and cruel

She-Wolves: The Women who ruled England before Elizabeth by Dr Helen Castor develops the theme of how women in England who held power were constrained by perceptions of women's right, and fitness to rule. She shows how Mary dealt with the societal paradigm in which she lived – basically by acting like any male sovereign, whilst paying lip-service to ideals of wifely obedience and feminine weakness. Whilst many portrayals of Elizabeth's success show her as learning from Mary's mistakes, Dr Castor's analysis suggests that Elizabeth learnt just as much from Mary's strengths.

Mary in Fiction

Mary is almost always a bit-part player in historical fiction – usually portrayed as the dowdy older sister to Elizabeth, as in Margaret Irwin's immensely influential trilogy *Young Bess, The Captive Princess and Elizabeth and the Prince of Spain*, or as a bitter, hysterical woman, brooding on her wrongs in Jean Plaidy's various works.

In Hilary Mantel's *Wolf Hall* and *Bring up the Bodies*, Mary is a minor character, for whom Cromwell seems to feel a rather superior sympathy.

In the 1970s, Hilda Lewis wrote a trilogy (*I am Mary Tudor; Mary the Queen; Bloody Mary*) about Mary which is, sadly, out of print. It is beautifully written and a broadly sympathetic portrait, although the last volume does focus very strongly on Mary as an hysterically jealous wife – I would guess it was modelled on H F M Prescott's biography of 1941.

Suzannah Dunn's *The Queen's Sorrow* is a much more recent novel, which is a gripping, although rather disturbing read.

Chapter 15: Book Review

Mary has been the subject of several modern biographies, and some interesting collections of essays, as summarised in the previous chapter. We have reviewed one of the collections of essays, that edited by Susan Doran and Thomas Freeman, here.

Title: Mary Tudor: Old and New Perspectives

Editors: Susan Doran and Thomas S Freeman

Publisher: Palgrave Macmillan

In a nutshell A series of thought-provoking essays which critically examine some of the perceptions about the life and reign of Mary I, England's first Queen-regnant.

Until the last ten years, almost all accounts of the reign of Mary I have been overwhelmingly negative. Beginning with John Foxe's *Acts and Monuments* in the 1570s, analysis has focused largely on the religious persecution of her reign. Even after the worst excesses of Protestant propaganda began to be peeled back in the more moderate accounts of the twentieth century, '*Bloody Mary*' has merely been replaced with '*Tragic Mary*', brooding bitterly on the wrongs done to her mother. This set of eleven essays makes a refreshing change by focusing on a range of aspects of the Queen's life and reign and how they were perceived, both at the time and later.

The writers are all academics with impressive qualifications. The editors, Dr Susan Doran and Dr Thomas Freeman (who also each contributed an essay) are Senior Research Fellow at Jesus College, Oxford, and Lecturer at the Faculty of Divinity at Cambridge University, respectively.

The book is divided into two parts – the first contains five essays that focus on the historic perceptions, including by Elizabeth Protestants who saw her as the antichrist, Elizabethan Catholics who perceived her as a saint, the Whig historians of the eighteenth century and a very interesting review of the perceptions of Mary by Jacobean playwrights (much less negative than you might think).

The second section looks at the new analysis and research from the last twenty years. Two related chapters look at Mary's education in the Humanist fashion of the 1520s, and how this played out in the translation project of Erasmus' *Paraphrases of the Gospels* patronised by Mary's step-mother, Katherine Parr, in which Mary undertook St John.

In an insightful chapter by Thomas Betteridge, Professor of Early Modern English Literature & Drama at Oxford Brookes University, he looks at how Mary's supporters and opponents used her gender as a political weapon, albeit in different ways. Her femininity could be seen as a positive attribute, emphasising the qualities of gentleness and mercy, whilst the individual circumstance of her failure to bear children was used to denigrate her as a woman and a queen.

Two chapters look at Mary's religious policy – one emphasising the positive aspects of the reintroduction of Catholicism – the patronage of the universities, the insistence on motivated, trained and virtuous parish clergy, the legacy of a reinvigorated musical tradition still a feature of Anglican worship, the other recounting in detail the extent of the religious persecution and the level of Mary's personal responsibility.

The final chapter, by Dr. Judith M Richards, draws together old and new interpretations of Mary's life and reign into a coherent whole – balancing the positive and the negative into a rounded portrait which steers a reasoned course between blind polemic accusations against the Queen, and partisan apologia.

Bibliography

Baldwin Smith, Lacey, '*The Last Will and Testament of Henry VIII: A Question of Perspective*', by Cambridge University Press on behalf of The North American Conference on British Studies, *Journal of British Studies*, Vol 2, Number 1 (1962), pp 14–27 http://www.jstor.org/stable/175305

Borman, Tracy, *Thomas Cromwell: The Untold Story of Henry VIII's Most Faithful Servant* (United Kingdom: Hodder & Stoughton, 2015)

Brewer, John Sherren, and James Gairdner, *Letters and Papers, Foreign and Domestic, of the Reign of Henry VIII: Preserved in the Public Record Office, the British Museum, and Elsewhere in Engl* (United Kingdom: British History Online, 2014)

'*Calendar of State Papers: Venice*' <http://www.british-history.ac.uk/cal-state-papers/venice/vol2/vii-lxi> [accessed 7 October 2015]

De Lisle, Leanda, *Tudor: The Family Story* (United Kingdom: Chatto & Windus, 2013)

Edwards, John, *Mary I: England's Catholic Queen* (New Haven: Yale University Press, 2011)

Ellis, Henry, *Original Letters, Illustrative of English History: Including Numerous Royal Letters: From Autographs in the British Museum, the State Paper Office, and One or Two Other Collections.*, 1st edn (New York: Printed for Harding, Triphook, & Lepard, 1824)

Hayward, Maria, ed., *The Great Wardrobe Accounts of Henry VII and Henry VIII* (United Kingdom: London Record Society, 2012)

Ives, Eric, *Lady Jane Grey: A Tudor Mystery*, 1st edn (United Kingdom: Wiley-Blackwell (an imprint of John Wiley & Sons Ltd), 2012)

Lipscomb, Dr Suzannah, *The King Is Dead* (United Kingdom: Head of Zeus, 2015)

Office, Public Record, *Calendar of State Papers: Domestic: Mary I 1553-1558* (London: Public Record Office, 1998)

Perspectives, New, *Mary Tudor: Old and New Perspectives (Hardback)*, ed. by Susan Doran and Thomas S. Freeman, Kindle (Basingstoke: Palgrave MacMillan, United Kingdom, 2011)

Pierce, Hazel, *Margaret Pole, Countess of Salisbury: 1473 - 1541: Loyalty, Lineage and Leadership* (Cardiff: University of Wales Press, 2009)

Porter, Dr Linda, *Mary Tudor: The First Queen* (London: Piatkus Books, 2009)

Tremlett, Giles, *Catherine of Aragon: Henry's Spanish Queen. by Giles Tremlett* (London: Faber and Faber, 2010)

Whitelock, Dr Anna, and Alice Hunt, eds., *Tudor Queenship: The Reigns of Mary and Elizabeth*, Kindle (Basingstoke: Palgrave Macmillan, 2012)

Whitelock, Dr Anna, *Mary Tudor: Princess, Bastard, Queen*, 1st edn (New York: Random House Publishing Group, 2010)

www.ingramcontent.com/pod-product-compliance
Lightning Source LLC
Chambersburg PA
CBHW020517030426
42337CB00011B/429